OFF ON OUR OWN

OFF ON OUR OWN

LIVING OFF-GRID IN
COMFORTABLE INDEPENDENCE

TED CARNS

Off On Our Own
Living Off-Grid in Comfortable Independence

Copyright © 2011 by Ted Carns

ISBN-13: 978-0-9832726-0-1

Library of Congress Control Number: 2011928753
CIP information available upon request

St. Lynn's Press. POB 18680. Pittsburgh, PA 15236
412.466.0790. www.stlynnspress.com

Cover Design – Heidi Spurgin, Pure Design
Book Design – Holly Rosborough, Network Printing Services
Editor – Catherine Dees

Photos on pages 104, 235, author photo on page 274, and
photos on front and back covers by Joni Koynok; photos on page 2
by Mark Ohi; all other photos courtesy of the author.

Printed in The United States of America –
in a facility certified FSC® and SFI®

This title and all of St. Lynn's Press books may be purchased for
educational, business, or sales promotional use.
For information please write:

Special Markets Department, St. Lynn's Press,
POB 18680, Pittsburgh, PA 15236

10 9 8 7 6 5 4 3 2 1

DEDICATION

To Mary, that would be Jesus's mom, to whom as a non-Catholic, non-Orthodox alien to the church I dedicate my life. For Her I resisted 532 impulses to use the "f-word" in reference to those forces in our culture that lead us to undermine, weaken and destroy the majestic equilibrium of nature. It's not that I worship nature before the Godhead, or tangible creation more than an intangible Creator – but rather that I see so clearly, "As we do, so is it done unto us."

As I try to walk the fine line between dominion and stewardship, I know that the quintessential mother of us all is fully aware of my efforts. So here's my disclaimer: When my words are true, they can be attributed to Her inspiration; when I get it wrong, it's all on me.

TABLE OF CONTENTS

EPILOGUE

INTRODUCTION

"...a simple life that works."

ℐℓℯ

A woman came by one afternoon a while back to talk with my soon-to-be wife about catering our wedding. She had brought her brother along to meet us. He was some sort of businessman who had just flown up from the south to visit her. When they got here I was locked in an emergency plumbing crisis, the water to the house was shut off and there were tools scattered everywhere. I apologized and encouraged the brother to go have a look around until I could be a proper host.

While the women were working and I was otherwise occupied, he went off on a self-guided tour of our place. There was a lot for him to see. Now it also happened that the previous day he had had a chance to tour one of the wealthiest estates in the valley below.

Time passed. I finally got the crisis under control and turned the water back on to the house. I looked over at the upper patio where Kathy and her friend were sitting and saw that they were closing their notebooks. I set out to let the brother know things were winding down at the house and maybe show him some of the things we love most about living here.

Later, as we were all saying goodbye and heading out to the gate, the young man turned to me and said with genuine feeling, "You know, yesterday I saw how the richest man lives, in great detail, and today I come here. I just have to tell you what I've concluded from these two experiences. Not only do you have what the rich man has, you have what he wishes he had but he never will."

Now, the funny thing about this very true story is that I'm probably one of the poorest men around, if all you're counting is dollars.

Kathy and I live on five acres adjoining my family's 46 acres in the rolling, forested hills of western Pennsylvania. The geography around us is defined by two parallel mountain ridges running north and south: Chestnut Ridge to the west and Laurel Mountain to the east. We're on the western side of Laurel at 2,000 feet elevation, a little above the frost line. In the evenings we watch the sun set on the Chestnut. Between the two mountains runs a long valley dotted with many towns, both rich and poor. Our place is on the old Forbes Trail, which has seen its share of American history.

Six miles due west of us is the town of Ligonier. That's where our farmers market and grocery are. The nearest big box stores are 17 miles further on. As for neighbors, the nearest are half a mile below, due west. But in the other 359 degrees surrounding us it's pretty much unsettled wilderness – miles and miles of it. We like it that way.

What the businessman-brother was responding to that day is what people often feel who experience The Stone Camp for the first time. They encounter two 21st century people who have chosen an independent, self-sufficient, self-sustaining way of living and in doing so have found a measure of true contentment.

There are two prominent aspects to our lives here, one having to do with what is unseen, the other with what is solid and three-dimensional. What is unseen is the way we co-exist with nature, which in turn blesses us with gifts too many to enumerate, most of them gifts for the spirit. The second aspect is what people see with their eyes when they come here: 15 buildings, more or less, including the main house, four guest houses, a summer kitchen, a sugar shack for making maple syrup, a chapel, a library and various storage sheds, two of which are like giant kitchen cupboards. One has place settings for 300-plus people and another has every type of manual and electric food processing tool you can imagine, plus all our canning and preserving equipment.

A visitor would also notice my "tool bus," an old converted school bus filled with parts and tools, and the vintage farm tractors – my workhorses – hooked up to various implements. It's not unusual to see a cat sitting motionless pretending to be a hood ornament. We have a sizable orchard, a huge garden, a small vineyard of purple and white Concord grapes, and Siberian kiwis, and berry patches everywhere. Some of the most important elements of The Stone Camp are not so easy to see, but they're there – the rainwater collection system and the gray water and black water processing systems, for example.

Through a series of small steps, learning as we went, Kathy and I have designed a lifestyle that can survive and flourish even if we were totally cut off. With a laughably small amount of money, we've created systems that will last well beyond our life-times. They guarantee our year-round comfort and insulate us from hunger, energy loss and even prolonged drought.

This book is about how it happened, why it happened and how anyone can cruise the archetypal avenue we're on, in what-ever way works best for them.

Now, Kathy and I love comfort as much as the next folks. We have most of the usual modern conveniences: fridge, freezer, washer, computer, cell phones, hot tub, vacuum, hair dryer, flat screen TV, stereo with surround sound – but we're not plugged into the power grid. Our house is wood-heated, we use solar and wind power, and we are in the process of weaning our vehicles entirely off of fossil fuels. We grow most of our own food, put up our harvest, make our own wine – and often drop fresh canned peaches into the solar-powered blender for our morning smooth-ies. It's a simple life that works: zero waste, total recycling, using systems that I invented and continue to invent, sometimes under the pressure of sheer, unavoidable necessity. I'll tell you how they all came about, the pleasures and the pains.

This is not a conventional how-to book. There are helpful how-to's already out there and the Internet has all the tech information you'd ever want – though you'll find a goodly number of creative projects here, both small and not-so-small. This book belongs to a category I'd call "how to how-to," meaning it introduces a way of thinking about solving problems, the kind that confront almost everyone who has a desire to live more simply, and successfully, in a complicated world. It really doesn't matter what your starting point is or how far you want to take it.

I'll also share some philosophical viewpoints that have evolved along with our lifestyle. Not too much, I hope. I'll try to warn you when I feel them coming on. You can't carve out a life like ours and not think about the deeper implications of things we choose to do as human beings.

Let me introduce you to The Stone Camp.

Madonna and Child in the woods

PART ONE

A Way of Life

Go confidently in the direction of your dreams.
Live the life you have imagined.

– Henry David Thoreau

The main house

The stone entryway

THE STONE CAMP

"...it was the hardest of possible conditions in which to carve out a true self-sufficient and self-sustaining lifestyle."

⌘

To be here is to be inside an 85-year-old living organism, rather than just a warm, cozy, inanimate house. Maybe conscious entity would be a better description. You'll see what I mean. But first, some history.

Way back in the family memory is a story of a grant of land being given in return for services to the old Forbes Trail around the time of the French and Indian War. The Forbes Trail was the vital link between British forts from Philadelphia to Pittsburgh. In our area it connected Ft. Bedford and Ft. Ligonier. Through the generations, the land was divided and divided again. In 1926 a 5-acre parcel was sold to some people from the city who wanted to have a hunting camp. They hired my great uncles to build it.

Great Uncle John, a master carpenter and woodwright,

headed up the project. They hauled materials up by mule train. To give a sense of how difficult that must have been, in the early '70s the Forest Service (now DCNR) told me The Stone Camp was the most isolated dwelling in Pennsylvania's southwest division.

The cabin was entirely framed in post-blighted wormy chestnut, most likely sawn on my Great Uncle Charley's steam-powered mill. I used to sit glued listening to the stories he told of the old days. He said he ordered the first chainsaw ever made, from Montgomery Ward's. I especially remember him telling me about the switch from crosscut saws and how fast that chainsaw cut the first big cherry tree he sunk it into.

This place came to be called The Stone Camp because it's entirely encased in mountain sandstone. You can tell it was probably done by the local family of stonemasons by the pattern they laid. It's a big family and these guys are still the best stonemasons around – and they're the nicest guys you'd ever meet. They were also good hunters, fishermen and trappers. They all had/have cool nicknames, like Fat, Spike, Heimy, Peg, Grummy Cork, Cocky, Lemon (his surname) and Ed, who never got nicknamed. I grew up with Bird and Big Liz (short for The Big Lizard). As far as I know, they could all do magic with mountain stone, but old Spike was one of the best.

By the time I came along years later and tried to dig a deep cistern, I found to my surprise that The Stone Camp doesn't sit on a concrete foundation. There's solid rock shelf about four feet down. The mortared stone encasement walls of the camp were set on a great, thick three-foot-wide, four-foot-high solid wall of stone and mortar. That huge foundation wall sits on a bed of sandstone crushed fine by hand with sledgehammers, that in turn sits on solid rock. I think the idea of the pulverized sandstone was to French-drain the entire foundation down the mountain so the freeze thaw wouldn't heave the walls.

It's an unusual way of building a stone house but it's lasted this long. I think of the parable of the wise man and the fool. It's said that the wise man builds his house on solid rock and the foolish man builds his on sand. Being that this house is built on both I guess I can claim the right to be both wise and foolish.

I once asked Great Uncle Charley where they got the water for the camp. He said there's a spring right over the hill that they all used. I couldn't find it for at least the first 25 years up here, the reason being that "right over the hill" to a guy who walked several miles to school is different to a guy who walked 75 yards to catch the bus. Turns out I was looking way too close. Finally I found it and sure enough, there was an old cut glass tumbler sticking out of the mud. The glass my ancestors used to drink from.

I remember coming up here as a child. The road seemed to wind uphill forever. Dad let us ride in the bed of the old teal-colored Chevy pickup. The wheels disappeared in the tall mountain grass and it gave us the distinct feeling the truck was floating like a boat through deep water. At the camp, Dad would talk to the hunters about which bucks were moving where and at what time of the day. There was a big black snake that was almost always sunning itself above the door that faced south. His descendants are still around and they often drop in for a visit.

Over time, people stopped coming to The Stone Camp and things began to deteriorate. The rain barrels rusted down to half their height. The place seemed abandoned, unwanted, the last place on earth anybody would ever want to live. There were no utilities, no water, no power; no soil, only rock and clay. There was no way to heat the main cabin but with a big, inefficient fireplace that constantly smoked. Lone Cabin Jr., now our main guesthouse, is where the hunters used to sleep. It had an old, ornate potbelly stove that some bastard has since stolen from us. The Stone Camp was truly the least among dwellings; it had nowhere to go but up.

Years passed, and it was pretty much forgotten – until one day a 19-year-old kid crawled through a broken window on two hits of purple microdot LSD. Somewhere in his (my) young mind was stored an image from an old movie: the warm, inviting cabin of Heidi's grandfather. I looked around and there I was, in Grandfather's cabin in the Alps, with the LSD making sure that warm feeling stuck. I fell completely in love with the place and arranged to move in, rent: $5 a month. The nice widow from the city who owned it said I could improve it any way I wanted, so every three months I would send her an update on my projects, along with a rent check.

In those days I wasn't bound by any builder's code (and to this day no insurance regulation). Being that I hated anything that had to do with conformity, I took my first step on a journey away from conventional living, and drugs as well, and into years of intense spiritual practices. I tried as best I could to imitate the lives of the hermits and sages.

When I look back I'm a bit embarrassed at myself. I was like a kid in a sandbox of spiritual traditions, but more of an immature, irresponsible, spiritual flunky than the sage I dreamed of becoming. I feel like I never perfected a single practice, but as the real masters say, the actual practices are worthless, but you gotta do the practices in order to see they're worthless. Once you finally realize there's nothing you can do, only then are you qualified to give up totally and surrender.

However, being so irresponsible does have its advantages. I was free to flip convention the bird and resurrect my childhood imagination into a lifestyle. I think that's what makes children's faces light up when they come here. There's so much Peter Pan stuff for them to do and look at. I once heard a youngster say, "This is way better than Disney World."

As far as wants, dreams and desires go, I probably have as many as anyone else. I just let go and watch my mind toy with its wishes, as a mother would let her child play with his new toy fire truck.

The good mother knows her child is in for a life of ups and downs, joys and sorrows. She sees the value of both, doesn't interfere, and just lets the kid entertain himself. She knows he'll either grow out of his pretend world or stay in it and become a real fireman.

A while back, I consented to a short interview on Finland's public television with two well-known Finnish environmentalists who came to see what The Stone Camp was all about. The first thing they said on camera was, "This place is like a fairyland but it's real." Another time an art teacher from New York said it's an example of "living art."

How did it happen? How did it go from the lowest of dwellings to "living art"? How did it become the conscious entity that I know it to be? It didn't happen all at once or from some pre-set plan. But it did have a lot to do with having Kathy in my life.

Kathy

Kathy and I went to the same high school. I was a year ahead of her. I don't think we ever said a word to each other but I do remember thinking, She has pretty legs. We actually met at a place called Heavenly Foods in 1976. She was hanging out with the guy who owned it but they weren't really involved. I invited them both to the mountain for dinner and then later asked her if she'd like to go for a hike. Next thing you know, three years later we were looking for a Christmas tree and I said, "Hey, come look at this one, it's already decorated." I had hung an engagement ring on one of the limbs and when she finally saw it I said, "Will you marry me?"

Seventeen years later and a lot of ups and downs, we built our own chapel and tied the knot. I dressed as an Indian; my hair was long and two little girls braided it and tied feathers and beads on the braids. Kathy dressed in half the time in a simple cotton dress and a wide-brim hat. She looked like a young girl from "Little House on the Prairie" on her way to a Sunday meeting. I'll let her tell her version of things.

Kathy: I grew up in the little town of Ligonier near here. I always loved the woods and forests but rarely spent time in them growing up. I tried to join the Peace Corps but was denied because I lacked the skills they were looking for. For myself, I wanted to live a simple lifestyle that did not require a lot of money. This area had a lot of small cabins and summer homes dotted around the hills, without plumbing and electricity. I knew of several guys my age who had moved into some of

Just married

these and were living there year round. It fascinated me that they could live like this.

Then I met Teddy, who was getting ready to move into The Stone Camp. My first experience here was when it was still a small stone cabin in the woods, no conveniences whatsoever. The only previous tenant had been a Norwegian wood rat who played havoc with anything and everything inside, so it was not anything like what people see who walk in now. I remember when Teddy killed the rat. It was deer hunting season and he took it down to his dad's hunting camp and hung it on the rack alongside the deer his family had gotten.

In those early days I would stay here alone when Teddy traveled. There were no cell phones, no radio or TV, and at that time no dogs or cats. The road was not in good condition, so I would park a half-mile away and walk up.

When Teddy did not commit to an actual wedding date I applied and went to West Virginia University for my master's in social work. Afterwards, I moved back to this area and started working. I bought a small cabin that the neighbors were trying to get torn down because it was condemned. My brother and Teddy said it was salvageable. We still own it and rent it out. While it was being remodeled I lived with Teddy for about a year, worked full-time and spent a lot of time here helping with whatever project was underway. It seemed every vacation I had from work I spent mixing and carrying cement.

There was a period in there when Teddy and I split for a while, but we had a dog named Pickles that we shared custody of, so that kept us in contact with each other. When we got back together he would say many times that I needed to quit my job to see what it took to live off-grid in a sustainable lifestyle. I told him I needed to save a little more money first. Then my mother died suddenly and a year later a brother died. I realized then that if I did not quit my job and see what it took to live this lifestyle, and something happened to Teddy, I would regret it forever – so I gave notice.

That was in 1993. Since then, it has all come together to be what it is today. I didn't work for a couple of years at first, then when I was accidentally dumped out of the back of our truck with a load of sawmill logs while we were trying to earn some money, I told Teddy I can make money without getting killed. So I went to work part-time for a while, eventually working full time in a nursing home in Ligonier, where I've been for the last ten years.

Those early years I loved to camp, so it was not so difficult living here. And we were young. Now, I really appreciate the indoor plumbing, not using the outhouse in the middle of the night, the cold toilet seat. The house is warm in the winter. I think we have all the necessities.

* * *

My childhood was a little different from Kathy's, except for the part about loving the woods and wanting to live simply. I grew up at the base of the Laurel Ridge. Old Route 30 runs through the town and then heads east up over the mountain. It's a treacherous descent for truckers. Before semi trucks got air brakes the people in our town were always on the alert for a spilled load from a truck wreck. I remember coming home from school one day and Dad saying, "Go down and see what's in the basement." It was filled with huge clusters of bananas. They hung from the ceiling almost down to the floor. If a truck wrecked, it was all fair game. I remember potatoes, fruit, sugar and even 55-gallon drums of highway paint. Waste wasn't something people believed in back then.

While most parents sent their kids to the local pool or amusement park for the summer, I was probably home helping Dad with something. Sometimes I envied my friends who had season passes and wondered, Doesn't your dad make you work? Don't you have to do stuff like get up in the middle of the night a couple times to trowel the fresh concrete on the basement floor to a sheen before it sets up? Half the time my friends had no idea what the hell I was talking about.

All I wanted to do was fish, catch snakes or else hike up the hill through the forest to where the wild grape vines grew. There I'd spend hours pretending I was Tarzan and perfecting his jungle call to Tantor and the elephant herd.

Working with Dad was as exciting as it was boring at times. It was out of diapers and into power tools. As soon as you lost interest in your baby rattle he handed you a Skilsaw. That's an exaggeration of course, but he did teach me a lot of adult work skills early in life.

Dad seemed intuitively aware and cautious. By having watched him over time I learned about every danger and how to avoid it. Then he'd hand me the tool, show me the switch, watch me cut a board or two and then walk away and let me try it on my own. Then when the summer passed, at least I could go back to school and brag a bit.

I used to watch people bring Dad broken watches and he'd tear them apart at the kitchen table with a coffee and a cigarette in his mouth. They'd bullshit about this and that, then he'd hand them back their watches, ticking. People who hunted up north would bring him a topo map. He'd look at it and say, "Stand here in the morning and there in the afternoon."

By my early teens I was a good welder. I hadn't even begun dreaming about a driver's license when Dad sat me on this huge WW2 airplane retriever we used to drag logs. It was essentially an army tank stripped of its turret and guns and armed with cable winches to drag wrecked planes off a runway ASAP. The darn thing would go about 30 mph full tilt. That was way more cool and fun than anything the other kids were doing.

Now I realize Dad gave me the best gift he could. From an early age he taught me the fundamentals of how to do almost anything. He set me in a mindset that erased the fears and intimidations most people have when they approach a task they weren't trained for. If I observed an intricate brain surgery technique three or four times I'd be itching for the scalpel.

Without knowing what he was doing, he planted the seeds of mystical creativity into my childhood brain. I don't recommend trying to do what my dad did with me because somebody would have you arrested for child endangerment. But I would like to share with you a little of what Dad breathed into my being. The gems of this mindset are scattered throughout this book.

The best I can describe The Stone Camp today is through other people's reactions. There was a little girl, Emily, who used to make a game of spotting what's new or changed between visits. Things change so rapidly here that when she hadn't visited for a time she had to start the game all over again. My wife's young niece Andrea walked in one time and said, "Aunt Kathy, nothing in your house matches, but it all goes together quite nicely."

In our guest book I was surprised to read the reaction of a boy who visited with The Westmoreland County Conservation School. He wrote: "If we are ever to colonize the moon or other planets, this is how we must learn to live."

Each year a group of students and staff from a well known university for the deaf comes to visit us for the weekend. I teach them wilderness survival techniques. One year I was in the house when the new students just arrived and I looked out the sunroom window to see a group of them sitting on the brick patio. That patio is where you first enter the grounds. They'd neither met me nor had they seen but a very tiny fraction of the place. All their hands seemed to be doing sign language at once and they all had intense expressions on their faces. I asked an interpreter what they were saying. He said, "Basically they all came to a sort of general consensus, having just this moment realized that we've all been deceived." He explained that they felt deceived about the American Dream. They got no argument from me. I believe that the compass for the so-called pursuit of happiness has been seriously mis-calibrated.

My buddy Jeff, who visits regularly, often spoke of The Stone Camp to his dad. I was boiling off maple syrup the day he finally brought his dad up to see the place. The sap was running and I couldn't spare much time to visit, so he showed his dad around. He told me later what his dad said: "You're right, it's almost impossible to describe…you have to see it for yourself."

About three miles away lived a man who was almost 100 years old. He was a living treasure chest of vivid memories – like when he pointed out to me where certain Indians had abducted a settler boy. One day I was cleaning the manure out of his barn with my backhoe. He leaned on the fence and watched me go in and out. The dump was nearly full, so I went over and said, "Ovie, wanna go for a ride?" "No thanks," he said, "never been more than 25 miles from home." I said, "It's only three miles."

Two loads later he came over and said, "I think maybe I will." I brought him up and gave him a two-bit tour. I showed him this and that and all the time I spoke he never said a word. I was thinking he forgot his hearing aid, but as we strolled back toward the truck he stopped, turned, looked me square in the eye and said, "Ripley himself wouldn't believe this unlessen he'd seen it." That was all he said.

I was to perform a wedding for a young couple from England who were educated in the Waldorf School System. It's founded on the principles and teachings of Rudolph Steiner. At the wedding were three generations from the Waldorf tradition. An entourage of their family and friends arrived to attend the wedding very early Saturday morning after a long night's drive. Seeing that no one was up and about, they walked around the grounds and checked out the chapel. I was still asleep on the living room couch when they finally ventured into the house. I was suddenly awakened to a room full of people I had never met. One man said, "Ah, now we see that Utopia actually does exist."

When I really stand back and reflect on what this place was and what it has become, I realize it was the hardest of possible conditions in which to carve out a true self-sufficient and self-sustaining lifestyle. And it was accomplished through necessity taking precedence over desire.

Before you turn the page, Kathy wants me to be sure to tell you that three years ago we bought back the land from the family that had owned it since 1926. It was always our home, but we just made it legal.

The chapel

Inside the chapel

2

NEEDS, DESIRES AND MAGIC

"I've come to believe that life works for us and with us..."

♻

Ours is a story about necessity becoming an art form. Because I refused the paycheck I was forced to focus on necessity. And because of that I just happened upon a certain magic. I was allowed to see what really happens when you have desires but can't pursue them beyond a slightly stretched arm's length.

My circumstance led me to simply reverse the equation we're all taught. More specifically, it made me reverse the "order of acquisition." What I soon saw was that if one keeps focused on necessity, primarily using thought as a tool to accomplish only what needs to be done, then things happen and unfold differently.

We have the option either to use thought or to let thought use us. If you take control of the reins of thought you're inclined to follow the path of necessity. If you let yourself be the mule, desires take the reins and you're led down one dead-end path after another.

There's a strong force influencing us to become mules, with desires leading us here and there, everything in modern life telling us to pursue desires, to let them lead our lives, and to build our lives around them on credit. I came to see that what *needs* to be done is often the last thing we *want* to do. Doing what's necessary can be the hardest path to follow because it appears so boring, drab and un-self-fulfilling. Facing needs just seems to lead us to the next damn thing that needs to be done…if you look at it that way.

What I found was when I took the reins of thought and focused the mind completely on what truly *needs* to be done, I got a big surprise. All of my wants and desires, every single one of them, eventually got fulfilled without an ounce of anxiety or a loan payment book.

I discovered the formula for this magic in the early '70s. I wanted to return to the state of Washington to work for the summer but all I had was a 1941 Willys MB army jeep. It would go 50 mph if it was screaming. If I'd have driven it 3,000 miles I probably would have needed back surgery.

What I needed was a real car. I thought and thought what was the most economical and efficient thing I could drive across the country. I decided on a Volkswagen squareback. It's like a mini station wagon with excellent gas mileage. I was looking for a '66 or '67 because those were the pre-planned obsolescence years. I went all hell on a search for one. As I love to paint cars, I was ready to paint it my favorite color, off white or light tan.

I'd find one in crappy shape or just miss one in good shape or I'd find one way out of my price range. Finally I just said, "Screw it, I'll stay home for the summer."

I quit searching and within days I got a phone message at my parents' to call an elderly woman friend of mine, Ruth. I rang Ruth up and she said, "Teddy, I just got a new car and I didn't trade my old one in – how would you like it for a buck." I hadn't seen Ruth in a few years so in my head I pictured some huge old Buick rusting out at the seams. I said I'd come over for a look.

I got there, saw her new, bright yellow VW squareback and drooled. Then she led me around back to an off-white 1967 Volkswagen squareback with 13,000 original miles, price: $1.

When I say all desires get fulfilled, it ain't always pretty. I come from a family of horsemen. Great Uncle Eugene was a trick rider in the Roy Rogers rodeo circuit. When I got really into wanting a horse, I was offered three within a year or so. There was a lot to do to prepare to keep horses, so the offers went on hold. During that time I was out riding with my buddy Gary on one of his horses, a green broke Palomino who went nuts if he didn't lead. We had gone down a dead-end trail, so we both turned our horses around, but the very moment my horse realized he was second in line he turned into a bronco. He threw me straight up in the air and I came down on a beech tree root that grew out of the ground like a swamp "cyprus knee." It was in the shape of human fist. The damn thing hit the joint where my right femur connects to the pelvis and put the whole left side of my body out of whack. Five and a half weeks in a chair, with a trip to the bathroom the biggest challenge of my day – and I never wanted to even smell a horse ever again. Desire satisfied!

I've come to believe that life works for us and with us, and that the concept of providence has to do with providing what is necessary, rather than what is desired. It's a matter of coming into alignment with providence, or the will of Creation, if I can put it that way. You can see the fluidity of providence in the food chains, for example, where and how affluence and excess throw wrenches in its gears. But that's a philosophic discussion for another time.

Now I've said that sometimes our house feels like a conscious being. At times it acts so alive and aware, it's eerie. My electric shop has a small, glass-roofed bay window facing south. It's a commercial brand window that had a difficult, puzzling leak on the top frame that holds the glass. I kept meaning to get around to fixing it but it was really intimidating. This one had me stumped.

The roof above the window is covered with dark charcoal-colored shingles. I often lay warped candles on it when the sun is out, to warm them up so they can be straightened. But you've got to watch closely or they'll melt. One day I took a 2-foot-long warped candle out, set it on the roof and went on to something else and spaced out. The candle started to melt and it ran down and sealed the leak. It sure looked like the leaking window fixed itself. Things fix themselves quite often up here.

Another story: I was about to put a new roof on the house. I planned to use an under-layer sheet of ice and water shield. It's a tar-like substance that goes under the shingle, and it really seals the roof. I wanted to use so much that if you turned the house upside down it would float. I hadn't quite figured out the economics for acquiring that much of it.

Around that time, Kathy and I stopped at a trailhead parking facility just on the other side of the mountain to eat a picnic lunch. We parked somewhat out of sight, at the edge of the woods. A little time passed and we noticed a roofing company truck pull up a short distance away. They probably assumed our car was empty and we were gone hiking, because they took several rolls of this expensive ice guard from the truck bed, set them just inside the woods and took off. It sure looked to Kathy and me that these guys had pilfered it from a job they were on and were planning to pick it up later, so we thought it was fair game. Those rolls saved us a bunch of money, and now we have a house that might just float if you turned it upside-down.

A Different Reality

A quote that always intrigued me was from the philosopher William James. He said something like: *Apart from the reality we are living, there are other profoundly different realities, separated from us by the thinnest of films.* I always thought that sounded cool, but I have to admit I'm not exactly sure what he meant.

My guess is these strange new realities aren't fabrications. They don't just hang out there obscure and unattainable. I suspect they represent some possibility that could have been attained by a different choice. One simple external step in a new direction could easily effect profound change in our lives, which in turn would go on to effect some profound change within us.

Tubs as practical wall art

Old friends

Beauty in utility

Well-loved copper pots

If those different realities didn't apply to us, if they weren't an option, then why the hell would he mention them or question them, or even be aware of them or conceive of them? My guess is he's talking about realities that are accessible, and you can still change the direction of your step and thereby perhaps change everything.

This book is really about a kind of radical shift to a different reality that James may have been talking about. A radical but very simple shift and all that's involved is a simple decision, a first step. Any person can make it in the blink of an eye and immediately after that take the first infant step into an entirely new reality. A new light is shed upon everything, and your life changes. Now you're at peace, *and then* you do things, where before, you did things *hoping* to reach peace.

The total response to necessity is simply to do what needs to be done. I want whatever I want, desire what I wish for, I dream about flying a motorized paraglider, but I leave that to a higher will. I'll be damned if I'm gonna take out a loan. That's what my life is all about and I just stumbled on it through circumstance.

I wake up every day to choose between 25 different roads to excellent experience and 30 avenues to explore in pursuit of my independence. Not one of them requires a Porsche. I find in facing necessity that self-expression gains a unique and creative independence. It gets honed. Following desire does exactly the opposite.

Focus upon necessity brings a profound change and leads to a different reality. Desires are focused on the *future;* necessity is faced in the *moment.* That's the key to creativity. The key to being able to fix, do, build and invent things is right there in the *moment* you face a problem or task. When you learn to give a thing permission to fix itself – a task permission to complete itself – you are made to dwell in the moment, with your faculties on full alert. Then the task itself – the broken thing itself – becomes the supervisor. Your only responsibility is to hand it tools. Those tools are your own unique and innate talents set to rest upon common sense. Humble yourself in subservience to the job. Allow the job to do the job.

When you discover this magic for yourself, you become less and less intimidated by life's trials and labors, for now you have learned to work with things as opposed to against them. Have total faith in yourself. There are so many things we all can accomplish. There is so much we can do and so little that we cannot do. March forward with courage in yourself for you have found patience, you have met necessity. You have achieved the state of effortless effort. You have mystically penetrated to the heart of that saying: "Unless the Lord buildeth the house, the laborers work in vain."

Every one of us is a tool chest of potential packed to the brim. Some may be missing a few screwdrivers but they are blessed with an excellent array of metric wrenches. Therefore, if you need a screwdriver offer your wrenches. Humanity has enough to fix itself, but if we fail as individuals to realize our non-dividual humanity, what good are the tools? You can't wipe your ass with a crescent wrench.

It sure would be nice if we all abandoned desire and came to full focus on necessities. We'd all be yelling, "Hey, where's the energy crisis? … Hey, how come nobody's fighting? … Since when did everybody have health care? … Mind if I strip the drive train out of your Abrams Tank to make me a 27-foot-wide Rototiller?"

My personal spiritual, philosophical take on life is everywhere in this book, as you've already seen. If I don't touch on some of those aspects you could end up simply trying to replicate things I've done and that could be fraught with limitations. My hope is to spark your unique creativity, to set you off on your own inventions. I want you to succeed and not get led down dead-ends. People have often remarked that I've done so much, but that's not the case. I've just done one thing. I had one goal and focused all my efforts on it with relatively few sidetracks.

There's a whole lot of spiritual contemplation behind the torque of my wrench. It's about starting with baby steps. Everyone can take them and undergo a similar journey to a similar end, but see it expressed in an entirely unique way. Whatever inner self-independence/reliance/sufficiency I have achieved is reflected outward in my life. It colors everything I do. That, of course, coupled with a reverent stewardship. It's the formula that's important, and when you hit on it, you get to relax in a kind of self-propelled easy chair where magic happens and miracles are so commonplace you just smile at them, instead of jumping up and down screaming, "Look, did you see what just happened! Can you believe it!!!"

3

FROM FIRST LIGHT

"All I did was I refused to be told how to live."

∂⁄ρ

Let me lead you into a house where you climb trees instead of stairs, a house where toads, salamanders, newts, frogs and tiny ring neck snakes live and they aren't in cages. If you find a cricket outside you can bring it in and the frogs will eat it right out of your hand. You're in a house where you're elated if a katydid finds its way in through the window because night after night it'll lull you into a deep sleep with the sound it makes. You're in a three-story house with no inside staircases, where instead you zip up and down on tree trunks from the forest that grew on themselves firm, knobby handholds and foot rests. You're in a house where deer and a half-wolf once came in and out like people, and at least 17 species of wild animals have dwelt, both the invited and the uninvited. I haven't counted species lately.

I once knew a person who lived on a secluded beachfront property. She had had some serious medical scare and survived. I remember she said each morning she would go for a walk on the beach and make an effort to see something new, a new seashell or a bird or a flower growing in the dunes.

Life here is similar but it doesn't take much effort. From the moment I hear the first bird I perceive and sense change. My first duties take me outside, and opening the door is something akin to a surprise package. You don't know if you'll be screaming at deer, backing up from a bear or chasing a possum out of the chicken coop. All you know is that something new is gonna be waiting for you.

I'm usually up before Kathy, for two reasons. I maintain a drop-of-a-feather level of alertness all night, so I don't sleep soundly and she hasn't the option to nap at a whim during the day as I do. As day breaks I like to turn the news on low, softly rattle a few pots and pans and set the coffee water to heating so the stir of life coaxes her up to get ready to leave for work.

Most of the newness that enters my senses is both pleasant and subtle, but there's always a vague foreboding that keeps me from floating off into bliss. "What could go wrong?" to me is like a constant background noise that my ears don't see fit to call my brain to attention. It's much like a productive haunting that keeps me watchful and grounded, but it doesn't interfere with or dampen the enjoyment I get from a multi-colored columbine that has just flowered out of nowhere in some strange place. A brand new patch of painted trilliums that just blossomed can take my breath away. The other day I noticed a cluster of albino bluets amidst the large patch of common sky blue ones growing above Wayne's World (the summer kitchen).

The other morning I was on my way up there to the propane fridge to get the soy creamer we use in coffee and the smoothie I made for Kathy the day before, when a gentle breeze coming down the mountain filled my nostrils with the scented bloom of the Canada Mayflower, wild Lilies of the Valley.

I've usually un-bear-proofed everything at first light, a little before Kathy gets up or the dogs even stir. I hang out the bird feeders and set out the cats' food dishes, but I leave the chickens for Kathy to deal with because she likes to. If the dogs kept us up half the night howling and barking they're at the door before I get my shoes on. Their noses tell me every step the bear took whose smell wafted through the window at 2 am. That means I also walk out back to see if another wall of a shed was ripped open or a door torn off its hinges.

I used to let them out to chase the bears at night until I saw Bethany grab "Cousin Vinnie's" right back foot and saw him reel around to grab at her. Vinnie was a very, very large male bear with a big white V on his chest. He may have been the 900-pound one shot the past season a good distance from here. It had a V on its chest. Vinnie just wouldn't scare. He'd walk toward you even if you were screaming at him and he cost me $400, the price of the 357 Magnum I bought to shoot in the air and send him running.

Sometimes, as the dawn is just awakening, I water the outside potted plants, check how ripe the fruit is getting or just walk into the garden to see how much things have grown or

Kathy in the kitchen

*Our living room, with Kathy's favorite rocking chair
and sleeping dog*

A cozy sitting place

One of our critter family

been eaten by deer. My favorite mornings are when the Concord grapes and kiwis are ripe. They taste best when they're night-chilled.

Mountain mornings are brisk on into early summer, so on my way back to the house I sometimes grab a handful of logs for the cook stove and fire it up. I don't mean to heat the house, just a little bubble of radiant warmth where Kathy can pull up her mother's rocker, drink her coffee and read something. I catch the radiance from my throne (the heavily pillowed left side of the couch). Then in perfect synch, the sun comes up, the air warms and the stove goes out on its own. Of course in the winter we shovel the paths and tend to the wood-heating stove first thing.

After our customary kiss goodbye I usually read or write a little before I get to my work of keeping up the homestead. On Monday, Wednesday and Friday I do two-plus hours of morning yoga. Kathy goes to the Y to swim or workout sometimes before she punches in and sometimes after work she goes bike riding. She's an avid triathlete.

As you'll learn in this book I'm a stickler for doing what needs to be done. So the first thing I do to warm up my work machine is to look for small tasks that need doing and I complete them (complete is the operative word). I might bury the kitchen scraps in the sunroom so the red worms can turn them into our fertilizer. I might take the recycling back to the shed and sort it into categories. When I say recycling I'm not just referring to the numbered plastics, tin and aluminum cans and colored glass and paper. I'm talking everything from plastic wrap, worn out pens, cigarette butts and chewing gum – in other words everything that's not buried in the soil of the sunroom. The sunroom is the most important "organ" in the body of the house. It's strangely beautiful and one of the reasons people call this place magical. Much more about the sunroom as we go along.

This time of year I might siphon water from one rainwater storage cistern to another, or pump up to the main cistern uphill that pressurizes the house taps. If it's raining hard you often see me running around like a madman, dressed in a Western slicker and one of my wide-brimmed Chinese rice paddy hats that I picked up at the flea market for a paltry sum.

We live on a mountainside, so the main cistern works like a water tower, but it's all underground so it won't freeze. The spring water harvest is a big thing up here. There are cisterns and containers catching most all of the rainwater runoff from the roofs and there are hoses running everywhere to transfer and store it in larger cisterns. I also might need to head down the mountain to fill up the drinking water jugs from one of two springs we use.

One difference between most people and us is our approach to water. We are totally water conscious (electricity conscious as well). Our awareness and concern for water is about as heightened as you can get. Our mind is on it through its entire cycle from collection, filtration, tap, drain and effluent dispersion.

There's no "pipe to nowhere" here. The gray water is filtered and released perhaps as clean as it came in and the one-gallon toilet flush feeds a methane digester whose effluent trickles down through an aggregate filter that might make a state-approved sand mound seem like child's play. In our lifestyle you just don't leave the water running, like you just don't leave a light turned on for no reason.

I usually do the laundry during the day when the sun is high or the wind is blowing hard. In the evening Kathy hangs it in what we call the "Maytag room." That's the room that faces down the mountain. It has its own wood stove. We store everything out there that can withstand freeze-thaw cycles because we only heat it in the winter when we need to dry our clothes. In the past week we have transferred all primary recycling operations to this room from the shed out back.

Kathy and I split the dishwashing duties too. We try to ace the kitchen out at night, but often space it out because we're either too damn tired or have a good movie to watch. I often face some part of that task in the morning, like putting the dishes away or taking the plastic wrap off the drying racks we hang it on after washing. The hot water tap at the kitchen is only connected to the system that's heated by the wood stove that we heat the house with. In the summer you simply take a big teakettle down to the sunroom and draw from the solar hot water system.

At any rate, I look for small jobs to complete and that gives me the strength, swift-kick momentum and productive mindset I need to face the bigger, more involved projects. Right now I'm building a new chicken coop, hauling woodchips in the dump truck from the piles down below and stripping out clean aluminum to take to the scrap yard. I try to schedule some time to help my dad on his old Jeep. I've volunteered to do all the new body mounts for the new fiberglass body he got to replace the old rusted-out steel one.

I remember once asking a buddy how he was and what he'd been up to. He said, "Just looking for things to do to fill my days." I know I had a shocked look on my face. I think it's called cognitive dissonance when a concept just won't register.

An important part of my day is cartoon time. I'm currently addicted to "Word Girl." Past addictions included "Jonny Quest," "Jackie Chan," and "The Monkey King." Unless I'm really, really involved with something I drop everything at 4:25 pm and head to our 20-inch flat screen. By the way, at this very moment there's a fat jib jab (gray squirrel) at the window about 11 inches from me. You should watch the dogs when I whisper those two words: *jib jab.* Bethany howls like a coon dog on a scent.

Our days are in essence like everybody else's days, but to others it's kinda like how we view a foreign culture. The lives of the country folk on the south coast of Crete or the rolling hillsides of Italy looked to me like lives of simple, heavenly bliss, but they face challenge, success, defeat and dysfunction like everybody else. The magic I think I see in their lives is their norm, but it's my dreamy-eyed, romantic projection that's partly a mirage.

I did my best to solidify that mirage into being for our lives here and found it can be done but not sustained. We're all haunted inwardly by a fundamental sense of incompleteness that can easily fester into misery if we let it. Making an external change can numb or cover up drabness and normalcy for a time but you can't stay high on vacation forever. The low always creeps back in to re-establish balance and regain its influential status. Best to make it a friend, not a foe.

However! Grabbing a towel at 3 am to go out and sit in the hot tub under a bright star-lit sky is a sizable dose of heaven on earth. It knocks that bland creeper down a few pegs. Our life is one of extremes in both directions. Almost like controlled induced psychosis. All I did was I refused to be told how to live. I see right through peer pressure and TV commercials like they're transparent ghosts. In admitting the "monkey-see monkey-do" aspect of myself I relaxed my hand in the cookie jar and was able to draw it back out into freedom of movement. And at this very moment the two frogs in the sunroom must wholeheartedly agree because they're having one of the loudest, most enthusiastic conversations I ever heard them have. That's our life in a nutshell. This book is a pecan pie.

The entrance to our garden

4

Time, Money and My Jeweled Cape

"Quite a bit of what really goes on here is unbelievable."

☙

I don't deal with money that much. I have the equivalent of a Ph.D. in the art of salvage and most of my construction economy revolves around the huge personal hardware store I've collected over the years. I buy a 5-gallon bucket of nuts and bolts at the flea market for $2. I could pick two bolts out of those thousands that you'd go off and pay $5 for in the hardware store.

Most of my inventory of tools and materials was built through flea market purchases for half pennies on the dollar. If my interests can't evolve around what I have on stock and with what I can do with my own two hands, chances are it'll never get done or I'm just not interested. What most people would call my "junk" is really my palette.

A lot of people know me as a generous workaholic who constantly barters for things and rebuilds what most people throw away. My big old Oliver 66 row cropper, a tractor I converted to run on wood smoke, was just given to me by some kind friends. (I've got a lot to say about wood gasification later on.)

My wife brags that I can fix anything, but in my mind I feel like I can't fix anything. That keeps me in a perpetual state of feeling intimidated, of struggling that borders on pointless worry, but my brother-in-law says I only work well under pressure. So I constantly feel on the verge of defeat, and that sees to it I almost always win.

Kathy and I have been married now for about 15 years. She has a profession and works nine to five. She does agree that I'd survive without her income, but with it I'm blessed with medical insurance and expansion possibilities that are equally beneficial to the both of us. She also pays for the phone, Internet, car insurance and taxes, but don't get the impression I'm a "kept" man with a sugar momma and that I sit on my ass all day.

The paycheck from my labor provides electricity, hot and cold running water, a warm, cozy house, a huge self-sufficient garden, an orchard, wine to drink, as much maple syrup as your taste buds can stand and your choice of a relaxing hot tub or a Finnish sauna. It also provides a profound sense of independent security.

I take care of 15 buildings and cut wood for 17 functional fires on the mountain. They don't all burn at once, thank God. Those 17 fires service the syrup boilers, the distillery, the sauna, the hot tub, the Oliver, two wood-burning cook stoves and the many wood stoves that heat our buildings and guesthouses. I keep and help keep a total of eight big tractors and track machines running and repaired, a couple of trucks, a snowcat and an array of tools including the sawmill and the stone crusher. When I had a collection of 22 chainsaws I suddenly realized I was being eccentric.

Kathy also finances big-ticket items like the Staber washing machine and the propane refrigerator. Occasionally she'll buy me a nice used toy like an International 500 diesel crawler with a 4-way clam bucket and backhoe attachment. Over the years she bought me a Ford 801 with a front-end loader and a Ford Dexta diesel too. I think it's true, the only difference between men and boys is the price (and maybe weight) of their toys, but really, those tractors do work for us and they benefit others as well. I get $400 a month rent from an old condemned cottage her brother and I fixed up for her when we first met. With the rent I buy parts and accessories for my toys, some hardware now and then and I still have a little left over to splurge at the flea market.

I'm told The Stone Camp is a special place but it's hard for me to describe because I'm always here. I evolved right along with it, so it's my norm. I said to Kathy one day, "There's 360 degrees in a circle and I can turn around slowly and spot 360 things that need done, repaired or developed."

People constantly ask me what it's like to live in such a peaceful, utopian, idealistic, and heavenly setting. I tell them I'm like a man who had a plain black cape tied permanently around his neck in a world with no mirrors. Over the years people would drop by and sew jewels into it. Others would embroider it with beautiful filigree designs and still others would edge it with fancy knot work and macramé. The cape became so known for its beauty that people started to come by just to see it.

At first he loved the praise and enjoyed the admiration, but that got old real quick. After a while you started to see a wince on his face when people said nice things about his cape. He couldn't see what everybody else was seeing. No matter how quickly he'd turn to see his beautiful cape he could barely get a peek at the corner of it because it flowed around behind him quicker than he could get a look.

Now you might want to jump in your car and rush to see this place, but before you do let me tell you about the opposite end of the scale so as to curb your enthusiasm a bit. Amongst the steady entourage of people who happen by to visit from time to time are many dedicated, seasoned spiritual seekers. I call them "extreme yogis." Some of them refer to The Stone Camp as "The Fire." I really don't know what they're talking about. I can only repeat what people say and comment on what I observe happens to them here. It may be so bright here that just a slight tremor can send you over the brink into darkness. Kind of like tears turning to laughter.

I do find it odd that there are probably 300-plus images of the Blessed Virgin Mary in this house and most people don't even see one of them. It's no doubt because there's so much other stuff to look at, but 300? A short visit here seems to be cool for most people. Much more than six hours and the place can start to be more like a therapy session than a simple visit. Even the dreams people have here can be intense and meaning-ful. But when they wake up scared nightmare-shitless they tend to assume the dreams are prophetic. A close friend of ours has spent time with approximately 37 (his count) different spiritual teachers and masters in a number of monasteries and ashrams. He told me there's no place he's ever been that's been harder to endure – but he kept coming back. Dave passed on four months ago in India on the eve of his birthday, the night before he was to fly home and retire here with Kathy and me.

No place I know digs out and unearths internal b.s. more than The Stone Camp. It could be any of several things that cause this phenomenon. Personally, I think it may be Mary's immaculate presence. She's an earthquake to bullshit, like a magnifying glass to the things we'd rather not reveal to ourselves. Whatever it is, there have been very few people who have seemed totally immune. I see it in people who come to stay for two weeks and leave in two days. Some come for the whole summer and are gone in a week.

I often think that our human culture is no more than the evolution of sophisticated escape buttons. Any time the real truth starts to surface in our minds any time we're cornered to reflect on the construct of our self-denial, just push a button: Hop in the car, go shopping, turn on the tube or just grab a bottle, hit the chocolate or roll up a fat one. If I'm right, there's not only no buttons here, but it's a mirror wherever you look, in all directions.

I've witnessed some profound first impressions of this place and I've seen it put a match to many a person's self-created, New Age enlightenment map. I've seen people begin to weep when they walked through the door and they can't say why. I've seen groups of elderly Catholic women seeming to float through the yard proclaiming this to be a reflection of heaven. I heard a

*The outdoor kitchen cupboard which contains all
our food processing equipment*

*South side of the woodshed complex, with library
and summer kitchen*

West side of the woodshed, with sugar shack at rear left

Lone Cabin Jr, our upper main guest house

Catholic priest say, "Not since Assisi." A few have been instantly offended by the place. Rarest of all are those who appear to be totally indifferent – maybe three at most but I only remember two. Many have said, "This is the way life was intended to be" … "I want your life" … "I've touched base."

I felt a tinge of the same when visiting the remote regions of foreign countries where life appeared full and simple. It was especially powerful in Medjugorje, in the former Yugoslavia – and in the countryside on Mt. Athos, the peninsula jutting out in the North Aegean Sea, where 20 ancient Eastern Orthodox monasteries have been built into the living rock.

I'm not a mystic by nature. I look for the rational explanations for mysteries, miracles and the supernatural. I'm only wide-eyed, wordless and stunned when I'm forced to be. But in my life the search for the rational often proves futile. When I try to find a rational explanation for the experience that people have when they come here I think of Ben Franklin saying, "Any person having witnessed and tasted the life of the savage would not dream of returning to white society." It was also recorded that certain barricades were constructed not to keep Indians out but to keep whites from running away to join the tribe.

Delightful Necessity

Having grown up camping a lot, I remember the route of invention we traveled to make our campsite comfortable, convenient and downright delightful. It's a very certain path or way of thinking that pursues utility in sight of transiency, a semi-permanence in what is passing. The main compass of that route guided us on an expansion and elaboration of necessity. We dressed what's necessary with frills and filigree.

Transiency and necessity are like kissing cousins. When you know your mortality to the very core of your being, desires lose their power to grab your mind by the throat. Forget your mortality and you begin seeking the unnecessary. In truth, there is a point to necessity but there is no point in raw desires for excess. Necessity is like a deep water sailboat with a great rudder to guide it straight through random blustery winds. Cut off the rudder and you have a life of desire guided by random impulses.

I think The Stone Camp is like the ultimate delightful camp. It is a very high elaboration of necessity. I think in essence it's the same "Ben Franklin" phenomenon, only magnified to stunning. It is the "life of the savage" synthesized with modern convenience but with little compromise.

People instinctively yearn to live in harmony with the land whether they're aware of it or not, and whether they admit it or not. So how people react here may have a rational basis. There may be no spiritual or supernatural attraction whatever. But... when you see people begin to weep, begin to shiver – and I hear a recent visitor who'd just spent 12 years in the slammer say over and over, "This is one degree shy of heaven" – the rational brain starts to stutter. About a month ago a man claimed, "This place is the very center of the universe." And another walked in and said, "Wow – this reminds me of Willy Wonka's chocolate factory!" Go figure.

I don't experience any of that cool stuff. I'm just repeating what I've heard with my own ears and seen with my own eyes.

I'm making no claims. I mean, how could I or why should I? That's a sure path to insanity.

The Library

People who come here eventually discover the library. It didn't start out to be a library, it just kind of evolved. I built a room onto the side of my woodshed. It had no windows. I called it "my dark room." In one corner I had a soft couch-like little place with some pillows and blankets. That's where I'd go when I'd hit a low point and needed to recalibrate. I'd wrap up in blankets like a caterpillar in a cocoon and let myself work through the anguish. After that was over I'd walk back out glowing and at peace because I just came out of a reality check. It's that kind of place.

Once, a group of very troubled kids was brought up by their counselors. There was a severely autistic boy named Joey. He got drawn to my dark corner like tin to a magnet. No words, bribes or coaxing could get him to leave that place. They had to drag him out of there kicking and screaming and he kept on kicking and screaming to get back in for quite a time.

I've since installed a big skylight in that room and now it's the library – four walls filled to overflowing, desk heaped, and little extraneous stacks all over the place. I've told people it's my Internet connection. The big north wall has the most shelves and they're filled with spiritual texts of all religions and the works of their saints. The east and the south walls are the how-to, cooking, gardening and nature section. The west wall is everything else. There are a few classics, a big bunch of philosophy, a few college texts, a couple of novels and a nice section of children's books.

The religion section covers all bases, as does the nature section. Hell, I even have a book on identifying all the birds in Great Britain. But the how-to is the most impressive. I'd be surprised if the technical info on any subject relevant to living an essential lifestyle isn't there somewhere. The only trouble is you can't Google it. You gotta get your hands dirty and explore the shelves to get what you're looking for.

Later in the book I talk about our garden and how important my topsoil is to me. I hauled it in, and if I leave I'll haul it out. I think I can say the same about the library. As vividly as I remember the first little tiny garden Kathy and I planted – just a few square feet – I also remember the day I heard a story about the building of a personal library. I can remember the first few books I collected and where they sat, to the left of the fireplace on top of an old cabinet. That was about 34 years ago.

Between three and four thousand people have come up here to visit, alone or with a tour, from maybe 30 countries, but I'm not keeping count. I lent a doctor my hardback "Writings of Hippocrates," and later tried to figure out who I lent it to. I looked through the guest book and found almost forty doctors.

The amazing thing is that all of this has evolved by word of mouth. Friends bring friends who in turn become friends and bring more people and they become friends. It's like a Facebook page that both is and is not. Kathy and I have such an open door policy that our doors don't even lock. It got a bit much one hot

Sunday afternoon when we had 18 unannounced visitors and all I wanted to do was skinny dip in our little pool. Not that it wasn't nice to see everyone, but that sweltering heat...

Time

Now that we have email, a cell phone and the fact you're reading this book, we might have to change the open door policy a bit. If interest should happen to surge we may have to start scheduling some things so we can have our share of quiet time and still be welcoming hosts. I have noticed a decline in the drop by's, but I don't think it's because we're losing friends.

I think it's what the Hopi elders predicted of the last days. They said we're going to see two distinct and profound changes. Change #1 is that it's going to get really hot, and #2 is that time will accelerate. It will be like "Oh my God, it's Friday again!" That happens when you get older, but the elders said this will be different – everybody will experience it.

I wondered and pondered just how that could happen. Then I realized, yes, time really is relative just as Einstein said, and we each can choose between two distinct approaches to time. We can either be obsessed with efficiency and saving time, or...we can kick back, relax and *take* time, or just simply *make* time. Time doesn't expand in the obsession to save it – it does the opposite: It shrinks. Time may be money, but money has wings, and like time it flies away as fast as it can. Life is where time is. Its fullness is in taking time and making time. Life actually disappears when all you want to do is strive for quickness and efficiency. Saving time may actually be even killing time. How ironic can you get? The effort to save it makes you lose it. Time-saving efficiency gets you to your destination quicker, but that's what makes time accelerate.

On reflection, I can remember sitting with artists, actors, actresses, activists, acupuncturists, anarchists, autistic children, professional athletes and total assholes; Ayurvedic, homeopathic and naturopathic healers, chiropractors, surgeons, pediatricians, dentists and general practitioners. I've spoken with victims of cancer and HIV who were in their last days among the living.

I've been woken up at 3 am to be told, "I spent all my children's college savings on cocaine. What the hell am I going to do?" I've chatted with psychiatrists, psychologists, psychoanalysts and philosophers; child therapists and social workers; teachers, lawyers, outlaws, juvenile delinquents and law enforcement officers; musicians, poets and an opera singer who sang for the Pope; Catholic priests, Zen Buddhist priests, Jehovah's Witnesses and preachers of most every Christian faith, members of every race, creed and religion, and a man who knew Al Capone when he was a kid.

I've had coffee with saintly persons and embodiments of apparent evil, and sometimes both at once. I saw a guy who was an undercover narcotic agent for 25 years sit with a confessed heavy bud smoker like best friends. I remember the narc said something like, "Nobody's on duty up here." I've sat with servants, masters, seekers of Truth and compulsive liars. Visitors from all over the world have walked through The Stone Camp's unlocked doors. And I still don't know how most of them even found the place.

Unembellished Truths

There are a bunch of spiritual books on the market that I call embellished truths. They're like fictional spiritual wonder stories. Some authors even say right out front their work is fictional, but people still want to make religions out of them. I watch in amazement as cult followings develop around these well-worded fantasies. People have asked me if I'd had the Seventh Insight they read about. I want to say "Yeah, with my guru Mickey Mouse."

I will be so bold as to say that this book is quite the opposite. I feel the need to *un*-embellish what really goes on here. Other realms of experience and manifestation that are often fabricated and sensationalized actually do occur here, but I just don't talk about them because it's way too personal. Quite a bit of what really goes on here is unbelievable.

Here's one example that rests just this side of the untold experience border:

Sorry guys, but no one will ever convince me that "trophy hunting" is anything more than a passing crude and arrogant abomination. I was obsessing about it one time and was suddenly hit on the head by the hammer of my own moth and butterfly collection. It represented years of collecting and I actually went flush at the thought of what a hypocrite I was.

I took the collection of butterflies down from the wall, dug a small grave under the pines and gave them a proper burial. Then I begged God to forgive me for judging people. I kept the cecropia and luna moth specimens just a little while longer so I could admire them. I had a real hard time digging their grave because they were so big, beautiful and rare and because I'd never actually seen one up here at the house.

That night at about 2 am I was woken by a scratching on the screen of the window to the left of me. I thought it was a mouse. It kept scratching so I grabbed a flashlight. I walked over to the window and there was the biggest, most beautiful cecropia moth I had ever seen. Chills went up my spine. I thought it was a ghost. I actually pinched myself.

I admired it until my eyes started slipping closed, and went back to bed. Then maybe around 3 or 4 am the scratching started again. This time it came from the window on the right. I thought, "That beautiful cecropia in the prime of her short existence wants to be admired a bit more," so I got up walked over and there was the biggest, most beautiful luna moth I'd ever seen. This is a true, unembellished story, one of many I could relate. So imagine the ones I won't relate!

* * *

Note: If you want to skip ahead to the nuts and bolts and systems that make The Stone Camp function, be my guest, but if any of this stuff I've been talking about strikes a chord with you and your life, I invite you to keep reading for a while.

A corner of the library

Heidi – an expert in timelessness

5

Deep Connections

"One year I was barefoot from late spring snow to early fall snow."

If you're a Star Trek fan, life here becomes very much like the town in the episode "Far Point Station." The town itself appeared like any other town, made of inanimate buildings and streets, but the whole place was the "shape-shifting" flesh of one huge sentient being that was injured and forced to settle on the planet's surface.

Far Point Station was a highly evolved conscious entity that in form reacted symbiotically to fulfill people's thoughts and wishes. If you went into a fabric shop you found the cloth of your dreams on the rack you swear wasn't there a moment ago. If you yearned for a particular fruit ripened to a particular perfection you found it was there all along in your fruit bowl, but you just hadn't noticed it before. That is how life really wants to relate to us all, but our desire-based mindset stifles its effort.

Far Point Station is pure fantasy. Star Trek is science fiction. But the story behind it has some basis in reality. It was said that daily a crow flew overhead and dropped a nice crust of bread to St. Anthony for lunch and if he had a visitor it would drop two. Manna from heaven, feeding 5,000 with a couple loaves and fishes, water all of a sudden flowing from a rock to save Haggar and Ishmael in their banishment to the desert – it's all the same phenomenon.

There are volumes of such accounts recorded in the lives of the saints of all religions, east and west, that sound a lot like Far Point Station, not to mention the many personal "I gotta tell you about this miraculous thing that happened to me" stories that damn near everyone can relate.

The Stone Camp in particular is very much like that town through no calculated effort on my part. It's only because circumstance removed the yoke and whip from the hands of desires, bridled them and placed them all in their proper stall. Thus life provides necessity and fulfills desires for me much like Far Point Station. Ponder this in light of Christ speaking about how "the lilies of the field" are dressed while we're fretting about our wardrobe.

Up here I'm like nothing more than the townsperson who sits in Far Point's visitors center, the welcome committeeman who is paid room and board for his service. I'm nothing more than a street lamp, a liaison that gives light to The Stone Camp's character and some of its mysteries, but I'm also like a computer application that was programmed a little by genetics and a lot by environment and experience.

Another part I play here is something akin to a blood cell driven by a vision of ultimate security. I move the nutrients that feed the growth toward that security from one place to another. Then I apply them with wrenches, hammers, soldering guns and screws. My efforts are like a therapy that increases flow, circulation and efficiency. Blood cells don't contemplate or say much. They're much too busy working their butts off to reflect on the fact they're working their butts off.

Basically I just see something broke or something that needs to be done and I walk down to the tool bus (my retired school bus) for the parts and tools I need to do the job. That's the part my dad taught me. Another part was my Eagle Scout training that, when combined with a strong Protestant work ethic, results in something like "Be Prepared" on steroids. But the whole thing is capped off with a strong desire to know what is truly pleasing in the face of God as opposed to what the "preachers" told me.

The visionary aspect came in large part from a woman named Ruth Scott – that's the Ruth who let me have her old VW squareback for a buck – and from the trickle of Mohawk blood in my veins from a distant ancestor named Thayendanegea. You have to admit, that's a strange and intoxicating brew, maybe even dysfunctional!

Thayendanegea

Thayendanegea has many descendants around here and north of here in the Mohawk Valley, so I'm not exactly unique. Still, my connection to him feels personal and even mystical. Born in 1743, he was one of the great leaders of his people during turbulent times. His parents were Christian and his Christian name was Joseph. He was known by the British and the Colonists as Joseph Brant – an educated man who was honored by King George III, respected by George Washington and accused of savagery by the press of his time.

In the past I looked hard in the mirror and strained to see the Mohawk heritage in my face but couldn't see a trace. I only searched my reflection to see what many ethnically pure people spotted in an instant, like the elderly Jewish couple who had a summer cabin at the foot of the mountain and claimed it was very apparent. I remember sitting at a large communal meal in Medjugorje, Yugoslavia. I didn't know anybody and seldom heard a word of English, so I kept pretty much to myself. At one point someone asked me where I was from and what was my ancestry. When I mentioned I had some Mohawk blood the entire place erupted in words and expressions that were clearly confirmations. I asked the woman who interpreted for us, "What was that all about?" She said, "They all could see it in you."

The mystical connection that I surmised, or should I say fantasized, came from a book I'd read about Joseph Brant. It may be nothing, but it got my attention, nevertheless. I had already been practicing zero-waste years before I read that the one thing that sent Joseph into a rage was waste. Neither of us could bear to see any form of waste. It was another shock when I read that Joseph had built a tiny chapel in the forest within sight of his house. I, too, had done that.

But if there is a truly self-evident proof of my bloodline, it is what happened one pitch-black midnight in the forest. I was alone, walking barefoot to hone my senses. Some sort of large beast began to track my scent for a good while and it just kept getting closer and closer. I don't know what it was because it was dark beyond dark. It could have been just a big curious wild dog, because the coyotes hadn't settled in, bears were rare at that time and it made too much noise to be a big cat.

As I was walking backward I touched a large oak tree, sat down with my back against it and unsheathed my big knife, expecting the animal to pounce on me. I'd already approached the scared shitless level when I started to hear its breath sniffing. I was about to faint from fear and all of a sudden I plunged my knife into the earth beside me and roared, "I am Mohawk, most feared!"

There wasn't anything false or desperate in that moment. I know beyond a doubt the pussy-assed white man got scared out of his pants and passed out. I know I was left with, and touched, my Native American heritage. I felt them all in me, the entire fearless Mohawk collective.

You don't have to dive too deep into books to learn how Native Americans viewed themselves in relationship to the earth. They saw themselves so much belonging to the earth that the idea of land ownership "did not compute." The earth was their mother. She sustained them and they adored Her. The very idea of profit was foreign to them because their entire focus was upon necessity. I think the whites caused severe cognitive dissonance in the brains of the Red Man. When they saw the buffalo being massacred and the genocidal fate the white man wished upon them I don't think they could even comprehend that form of sanctioned blind malice, and that hampered their successful resistance to it.

Into the woods

Barefoot Walking

From an early age I had been addicted to David Carradine's Kung Fu character. Primitive skills were my prime fascination. I told myself from day one that these masters were no different from anybody else, they simply had an idea and then applied dedication and an extreme amount of practice. So I invented my own college with its own curriculum and shot for a Ph.D. in what interested me.

Maybe it's that drop of Mohawk in me, but I'm here to tell you that barefoot walking is a wonderful discipline and avenue of discovery. Walking barefoot at night is less painful than walking in daylight. That's because your eyes shift from their sockets to your feet. Your feet come alive like two little ninjas. They sense things your daylight eyes don't see, but they only turn on at night. And there's not a damn thing the brain in your head can do about it, because it's instinct.

Here on the mountain we're plagued with greenbriar thickets. Their thorny stems are not quite as bad as a rose stem but their tender green spring shoots rival asparagus in a stir-fry. In daylight I used to pick out a particularly thick area, one you'd avoid like the plague, and go back there barefoot in shorts when the stars came out. Then I'd do some deep breathing and enter the thicket like a cloud, move through it like a river that flows so slow you can't even tell there's a current. If you think you can imagine how slow I walked, cut that in half. At first I got pricked a lot. After a few years, if I got pricked even once it was unusual.

One year I was barefoot from late spring snow to early fall snow. I could hike if there were periodic patches of bare ground but not in a full snow. One of those years I swam in the pond every day all winter, save three days – that is, if you call a quick dive in, a few short underwater strokes and a quicker jump out for my towel and blanket an actual swim. I do remember that long barefoot year was also the year of the copperhead. My dog Beowulf got bit on the nose once. I wasn't afraid of stepping on them at night because of an observation I made when I was out with my three type-A un-neutered male monster dogs, Beowulf, Kokoki and Gustov. Beowulf was half wolf and half Malamute. The other two I'd gotten after Wulfie had been with me for several years – a full grown Malamute and a full grown Siberian husky. Kokoki and Gustov were both trouble dogs. Gustov, the husky, attacked people.

Running the forests and mountains with these three was storybook stuff of legend, but the slightest tremor would send them to one another's throats. Although Koko outweighed Beowulf by 15 or 20 pounds, Wulfie could pin him fast to the ground by his throat in about three seconds. Gustov was psycho and vicious but Wulfie could damn near blow him down with a breath. They got along for the most part. I just wouldn't let them fight.

I spotted a huge garter snake in the thick ferns one afternoon out where the dogs were romping. They kicked it and stepped on it many, many times in their play, but they didn't notice it was there. The whole time that snake never expressed a bit of aggressive defense. That went on for a while and then I called their attention to the snake and immediately when dog eyes met snake eyes it coiled, struck and displayed aggression. By that observation I walked fearlessly amidst the forest during a cyclic year of copperheads. It convinced me utterly that I would not get bit. And I didn't.

One year I took a 15-mile hike barefoot. That was a mistake. I didn't get cut; I strained my tendons and crawled the last half mile to the car. I pushed myself to extremes my first years alone in the mountain. I confronted fears I didn't even know I had before Beowulf became my companion.

Beowulf was at my side up here for 16 years. I got him near Beacon Rock about 50 miles east of Portland on the Washington side of the Columbia River. His mother was a caged wild wolf and his father was a champion Malamute sled dog. He was so valued for his genes that after being hit by a log truck they had part of his pelvis reconstructed with stainless steel so they could breed him. There were 12 in the litter. Six looked like their Malamute father and six like the mother wolf. I took the largest male whose characteristics were predominately wolf.

Beowulf could run down a deer and snap its neck. Yet, if I had a daycare center I would have left him alone with a dozen infants poking his eyes and pulling his ears. Little children called him "Wulfie Person." He and I lived a dream. But dreams end, and the day came when Wulfie died.

At that time Kathy and I had a crude and disjointed electrical system. Some things were battery operated, some on a main battery bank. I have no idea how the two events relate to one another, but the morning after he died we began to discover over the next few days that every electrical thing in the house just didn't work anymore. TV, radio, lights, tape deck, reverb and graphic equalizer – everything either fused internally or burned up mysteriously. Then we realized the entire huge battery bank was deader than a doornail. For years I thought it was his death agony, his spiritual release, and I still do. Some friends had another explanation. They suggested it was my X-Man release of emotions, the primal roar I let loose when I was told he was gone (I still laugh about that one).

Ruth

When I was a child my parents enrolled me in Powdermill Nature School. It was part of Carnegie Museum of Natural

History's Powdermill Nature Reserve, outside of Ligonier. Ruth Jury Scott was the resident environmental educator at the reserve through the '60s and '70s. She and Rachel Carson were close friends and confidantes who shared a deep concern for the harm that pesticide abuse was wreaking on the environment. Rachel Carson's 1962 book "Silent Spring" was really the beginning of the modern environmental movement.

To my own good fortune, Ruth zeroed in on me and kept me close into my late teens. She admitted to me years later that I reminded her of her late husband, J. Lewis Scott, "Scotty," who always had a laugh and a smile. He teased and kidded around incessantly. I remember giving her a 5 x 7 portrait of myself after I graduated and she was so upset that I wasn't smiling.

Ruth was one of the gentlest, most patient, wisest and strongest persons I ever met. She arranged finances to hire me for a summer after I graduated from high school. Each day she taught me all about a different plant. She turned me on to the study of ferns.

One of the last times I saw her she told me that the entire staff at Powdermill Nature School knew I had "it" in me, but she never really told me what "it" was. The very last time I went to see her in the nursing home I was forewarned she had totally lost her memory.

I walked into the room. She was sleeping in a chair. I bent down and whispered in her ear, "Ruth, it's Teddy," and I kissed her on the cheek. She opened her eyes and exclaimed with surprise and enthusiasm, "Teddy!" She had complete recognition for five or ten seconds, the transition between sleep and wakefulness, and then I saw the recognition quickly fade from her eyes. In her last years Kathy and I would visit her now and then. What amazed me was that, even as she gradually lost her mental clarity she still maintained a certain insight and commented on how she could see what Kathy and I represented together. She could perceive our environmental awareness and remarked how we stood out amongst others.

Rachel Carson and Ruth Scott

At the private ceremonial sprinkling of Ruth's ashes I was referred to three times as her son. The decision where to distribute her ashes was, "Ask Teddy." Yet, at the formal ceremony in Pittsburgh, no one was aware of our closeness. An environmental writer who worked with her on a biography of Rachel Carson said, "Ruth was a magical spirit who lived a life of absolute integrity. ...The world has lost a person who understood nature as few people ever have."

Ruth attempted to fill me with environmental sensitivities, but she couldn't keep me from catching, caging and playing with snakes, especially the huge black rat snakes. She knew me to almost always have one as a pet.

I brought some of her ashes home the day of the scattering, walked in and set them on the left side of the fireplace mantle. Then I turned and walked to the opposite end of the room and sat down at the dining table facing back across toward the fireplace. On the wall to the far left of the fireplace was a high shelf where I stored many bottles of holy water, Ganges water and water from springs where The Virgin Mary appeared to children. There were also boxes of rosaries, mala prayer beads, incense and religious medallions of all kinds.

I no sooner took a bite of lunch when we began to hear strange sounds coming from somewhere near the mantle. Kathy walked over and in a slightly alarmed voice said, "Teddy, look here." When I got to where she was standing, the high shelf began to shiver intensely and I looked up. There on the shelf were two enormous black rat snakes bound together sexually and enrapt in orgasmic ecstasy, thus the shiver. Ornate boxes, bottles and small urns came flying off the shelf to the floor. Yet not a single box opened to spill its contents, nor did a single bottle of holy water break or urn of frankincense or myrrh crystals empty on the floor.

When I reached up to take a snake in each hand neither expressed the slightest aggression or fear of me. It was as if they were fully sentient beings. I set them down outside under the pines and they slowly crawled off. As one of our cats came near and approached them, the second snake turned and struck at it like lightning. Make of it what you will.

6

Recycling

*"One of the main ecological principles in nature is that
every end is linked to a new beginning."*

I considered Ruth Scott to be an incarnation of Mother Nature,
so I was always trying to get her to utter some prophetic
words. Only twice did she take the bait. The first thing she said
was "Teddy, the mountains are more sacred than we can possibly
imagine. They are our stability in so many ways, especially in
regulating the weather patterns. They were severely exploited at
the turn of the century. When you see the second exploitation of
the mountains, know that the collapse of civilization's paradigm
as we know it is imminent."

We're advised to treat people as we would have them treat
us. How the hell that same rule wouldn't apply to our treatment
of the environment is beyond me. I think what Ruth was saying in a nutshell was: Do unto creation as you would have it do
unto you, for as you sow, so shall you reap. And if you don't come

down off your delusionary dominion pedestal she'll just plain knock you off. She'll burn, starve, freeze, flood, or blow you away with a strong wind.

In Pennsylvania, from where I sit, the second exploitation is near to complete. By the hand of the state government and whoever has the money, it has now encompassed me on all sides. It is even doubling back on itself in order to squeeze the last ounce of timber "resource" that it can. First it partial-cut and now it has justified clear-cutting the same places it partial-cut. Now everybody's going all hog for the natural gas. It's the new "too good to be true" goose-with-the-golden-egg rush. Every time I turn around another neighbor has sold out his gas rights. Poor Pennsylvania. We drew out the oil and coal, burned it and destroyed the atmosphere. We let the timber barons rape the entire landscape except the few virgin acres that they had the audacity to set aside and name after themselves. And now were fracking what's underneath us with chemicals that, as of this writing, the gas companies aren't even required to disclose. And it looks like we won't stop till we've destroyed what's above us, around, before and beneath us as well.

The second thing Ruth told me was, "Until man's economy comes to mimic ecological principles, civilizations will continue to arise and collapse." In my theological search for why, I came to realize that an economy disobedient to ecological principles is just one of many complications of a single and original act of disobedience. Something ingrained in our nature, whatever that might be, forged us a permission slip to take what we can take and not stop until there's no more to take.

Mimicking ecological principles may hold the key to our chance to survive as a race and to leave something for our kids as well. One of the main ecological principles in nature is that every end is linked to a new beginning. That principle can be condensed into a single word, and that word is…recycling.

I see recycling as one of the most important ecological principles that our civilization can engage in directly. It is a tangible, hands-on thing we each can do. It may be the therapy needed to restore our lost sanity and the health of the ecosystem as well, if indeed the two even differ. I personally believe the state of our ecology and the state of our minds reciprocate utterly and perfectly.

I don't see how a civilization founded on ecological principles could possibly fail if its vanity can be kept from overshadowing the practice. We are starting to recycle more, but it still has a stigma to overcome. Statistics show that most people tend to trivialize it. In a lot of minds it just gets pigeon-holed in their mental dungeon so tofu has somebody to talk with – tofu, the highly efficient protein source that gets laughs instead of its due reverence. Now that's stigmatizing!

Recycling is a miracle therapy that deserves better from us, because by tapping directly into the waste stream we reconnect the broken circle of life. The waste stream may be the most efficient self-sustaining economic protein source there is in life.

A true story: It happened that I was walking through the pines in the front of the house and noticed a bird's nest that had fallen on the ground. I picked it up and was struck by how soft it was inside. I imagined how nice it was for the little peepees, the baby birds. I gently pulled out a bit of the lining to see what it actually was. It was my own hair. That experience planted the seed in my mind that grew into a vision of zero waste. It made me realize that total recycling really is one of the main ecological principles we need to be mimicking.

Rule #1: Every end must meet with a new beginning.
During the next 12 years I took to recycling like the eccentric madman that I am. My parents would whisper to my friends, *"He's really gone overboard this time."* What I could take to drop-off points and collection bins I did, but that was a small percentage of the "trash" I generated. That left me with a whole lot of stuff to deal with. Now, after 35 years, my zero waste operation is so extensive and complex it would take its own fat book to describe. But it would have to be constantly updated because the practice continues to change and evolve. I've managed to find innovative uses for almost everything, down to finding a use for cigarette butts. That wasn't a big problem because I don't smoke. In all these years I've only filled about half of a 2-gallon plastic bucket.

It happened that one afternoon I was sitting on the edge of a rock outcropping that dropped off like a small cliff. I noticed a strange little cocoon lodged in the crack of a huge flat rock that hung out over the edge. The cocoon was a brilliant white. I began to wonder why an insect would weave its home in such a vulnerable place. It was so exposed to the elements and every time it rained it surely got soaked by a runoff stream of water. My curiosity got the best of me, so I gently dislodged it and examined it closely. Its ends were rounded. It had no odor and no color. Eventually I gave up wondering what insect larvae might be inside and I flicked it over the cliff.

A bit later I remembered that hunters often use this overlook to spot deer down in Jack Hollow, so I scrambled down to see if I could find it again. I did and I tore it open with my fingernails. To my surprise there were no larvae inside. Sure enough, it was a cigarette butt – pure, synthetic plastic acetate with all trace of organic material washed out by the rain. Bingo! The butt birthed its reason to be.

Now it also happens that certain garden insect pests respond to nicotine spray. Which gave me a thought. I figured I could design a way to leach the nicotine out of those butts in my bucket without having to get my hands dirty. I thought this idea was original, but then I read about a center of sustainability in Australia that came up with the same idea. But the important thing is that I now knew how to give that butt end a new beginning – Rule #1. When I realized that the butt manifestation on the edge of the cliff could have been there for five, ten or fifteen years it led me to realize rule #2.

Rule #2: Time has no relevance in the practice of zero waste.

Mother Nature is patience supreme. She has plenty of time to grind the Alps into topsoil, so once the nicotine is leached out (and made into bug spray) I'll devote a short section of rain gutter to washing the butts cocoon-clean for the next ten, twenty or however many years it takes. If I need them sooner I'll step in and speed up the process. I'm sure I could use them to filter some non-potable liquid like a solvent or maybe use them in the process of making biodiesel. It makes no difference whether I've already done that or not. The important thing is the butts are slated for some use, given a new beginning. For now, they're quite content to sit, sealed in their 2-gallon plastic bucket.

I had already been practicing Rule #3, but the butt end experience drove it home.

Rule #3: All organic matter must be separated from all synthetic material.

That means our "garbage" is washed with the dishes. Sometimes our "garbage" even takes precedence over the dishes. An example of precedence is a plastic tub that stored oil cured olives. That tub may get the hottest, freshest water, because if there is even a trace of food left on any plastic container or bag, if there's so much as a tiny smear of chocolate left on a candy wrapper, it gets sent back to the kitchen from the recycling shed to get rewashed. Why? Because it can become nature's Petri dish, where all kinds of bacteria and undesirable things will grow.

I'll give you a little glimpse of the immensity that lies between the bird's nest and the cigarette butt. As paper bin recycling comes and goes in our communities, so does the way we deal with paper. Our warehouse out back used to have one room that was like a huge file cabinet. At one time we had 17 categories of paper, some of it saved for future usefulness, some destined to be recycled – including: waxed paper for fire-starting; paper that was best for actually soaking down and making paper (homemade paper is nice to wrap homemade soap in; also nice to make bookmarks); newsprint that used soy-based ink, for garden mulch (the other kind of newsprint went to farmers for bedding.); old greeting cards that could be cut up and made into new, homemade greeting cards; telephone books for their annual recycling; brown paper bags and unbleached paper; envelopes with windows (we would remove the windows in the event we found or heard of a town that was accepting office paper but required the windows be removed.); reusable wrapping paper; several categories of specific colored paper (strong blues, reds, oranges, greens etc.); old hardbacks to be broken down for recycling; magazines to be recycled (magazines of interest would go to the warehouse down at Dad's, for articles and collage.); scratch paper; cardboard boxes; padded envelopes... etc. etc.

So we'd amass these categories and then we'd watch for a town that had a collection, sometimes quite a distance away. We'd determine what they'd take, combine categories and haul a huge load of whatever. Now darn near everything is taken at the recycling center in town and we've cut back on the number of categories we keep tabs on.

Recycling can save you money in unexpected ways. It actually saved us around $125 in cash enclosed in birthday cards that would have rotted in the landfill had they not been subject to our reprocessing. I distinctly remember finding $75 in one envelope, and Kathy just reminded me also of a brown envelope

Ready for re-purposing

Cookie tins for holding various sizes of round recyclables

The tool bus, my converted old school bus

Some inventory in the tool bus

that contained several hundred dollars' worth of Lucent stock that got tossed but retrieved because of our process. My parents had divided their shares up among us kids when AT&T split. I sold mine in a hurry and came out ahead, while everyone else kept theirs as Lucent lost its value.

Consider caps. Right now we have six main cap categories and probably six or more sub-categories. Aluminum screw caps and tin lids from glass jars both go to the scrap yard. Mom saves aluminum can flip tabs and turns them in for fund-raiser credit. Tin beer and pop bottle caps, both the screw-off type and the ones that need an old-fashioned bottle opener, get tossed in the cement mixer to reinforce concrete. All common plastic caps are inventoried for use in a homemade fishpond filter modeled after a commercial one I bought at the flea market.

I also keep a Noah's Ark inventory of two or more of every cap of every size and dimension I ever came across. People actually come up here to access this inventory to replace caps that they lost. I also have the biggest inventory of assorted corks this side of the Mississippi. Synthetic wine corks get reused when I bottle my wine and mead. You may never have thought about the almost infinite variety of caps out there and their possible uses. In the category of smaller caps, there are soy, rice and almond milk caps, and a selection of every kind of aerosol spray can cap, stored in lacquer thinner. I keep a small inventory of different-sized aluminum foil yogurt lids. I fold one down around the top of Kathy's smoothie glass till she gets home. I also keep every type of shaker cap insert with different sizes and clusters of holes in them, the kind you'll see on jars of salt, pepper and other spices. I have a half-full cookie tin of those.

Shapes of things are important. In about 14 round cookie tins of various sizes I keep samples of every manmade material that is circular and two-dimensional. Those cookie tins hold every natural, synthesized and compound bonded material I ever came across, sized from a tiny coin up to the biggest, which may be about 10 inches across and ¼-inch thick: glass, Plexiglass, tin, aluminum, plastic, rubber, latex, silicon, wax-impregnated cardboard, wood and no doubt hundreds of bonded variations. There's even a round, glass bottom of a broken wine glass along with a couple old CD's. I have a similar inventory of square and rectangular materials in square cookie tins. I access both these inventories a lot, often for gaskets, BB or blowgun targets, or maybe I need a perfect circle of a certain size to use as a tracing pattern. Sometimes I might need a shim of say 15/1000 of an inch that is resistant to petroleum distillates. Do you get my drift? I call them my indexed resources.

I don't expect anyone else to even attempt my recycling system, I'm just telling you what mine looks like, as an example of how far you can take it and the security you feel when you know that you can create or fix pretty much anything once you've got the resources. In the warehouse down at Dad's place it gets really intense (my folks are those "nearest neighbors" I mentioned in my introduction, living about a half-mile down the hill from us). At Dad's warehouse there are, it seems, endless inventories of springs, hose clamps, nuts, bolts, cable clamps, turnbuckles, all manner of linkage, pulleys, exhaust pipe clamps, and exhaust pipe reducers. There's solid round stock, and hollow round stock, square stock, machined eyes, concrete anchors, a collection of electric motors and even two large tool boxes labeled Tech Shape #1 and Tech Shape #2.

It's endless, and out of all this half-cent on the dollar stash, I build stuff. Its mass is the palette that contains the colors I mix to create and invent my life. The hardware stores don't make much money from me.

In the Sunroom

The sunroom is built onto the southern exposure of the house. Later, in the Systems section of the book, I describe how the sunroom got built and go into detail about its multiple functions. It is the real living room of the house. I don't think there's another room like it anywhere.

In the light of recycling, you might say the sunroom handles most of the organic half of our effluent. The first two terraces as you walk down into it from our main living area are actual Mother Earth. I personally think there's something powerful in that fact, some indefinable kind of magic. I have heard people say that, in a way, the doors to our house don't exist because nature is "in here" as much as it is "out there." All of the organic waste that's generated in the kitchen with the exception of citrus peels has been buried in the sunroom's earth for the past 20-odd years. The composting red worms in that soil will consume a 2-gallon bucket of kitchen waste in about four weeks. Then we pack the worm castings (poop) in the legs of a pair of women's panty hose and suspend it in 55-gallon plastic drums of water. We use that liquid to fertilize our garden. You can spray it directly on foliage but it's so "hot" it has to be cut 10 to 1.

The sunroom is like a pre-fall reflection of Eden. A mated pair of beautiful milk snakes has their own underground private route in from outside. During dry, hot times in the summer the female comes in early in the morning and I hear her taking a swim with the fish and frogs. She bathes, gets a drink and then leaves. Sometimes if it's cold out she waits for the morning sun to soak up some heat before going back out. She is very elegant. In the morning sunlight her color and beadwork pattern are simply dazzling. Something tells me she and her stubby hubby (his tail got bit off) might have feasted on my anole lizards. I haven't seen them lately but then again anoles are chameleon, masters of camouflage, and it's something of a jungle down there. There are and have been toads, frogs, newts, anoles, salamanders, snakes, goldfish and a turtle. Even my pet boy deer liked to go down there to add some pee to the living soil.

Frogs and Toads

The frogs are an important part of our in-house ecosystem. They roam throughout the house at night keeping the insect population down. Often when we entertain people for dinner and wine we erupt into boisterous laughter. That sets the frogs to croaking and it seems like they too enjoyed the joke. But the clang of doing the dishes sets them to singing too, so that blows the theory that they have a sense of humor.

One night during a thunderstorm, Kathy and I were sitting

down there in the sunroom at the big stone slab table. There were torrential rains and fierce lightning. In my mind the windmill tower, right outside about 20 yards from us, was yelling, "Strike here, Strike me!" Kathy had on tennis shoes (rubber soles) and I was in my bare feet. I got real paranoid about getting electrocuted so I lifted both my feet up, rested my heels on the wooden chair rung to get them off the stone floor. I started counting seconds between the flash and the thunder. It was approaching two seconds, one second, a half-second and my toes were squirming nervous. Then came one big BOOM/FLASH and the huge, 10-square-foot, 2-inch thick stone table slab suddenly lifted a few inches off its stucco-ed brick pillar and came back down to rest with a hammering thud. One of those frogs had spied my squirming toes and thought one was a bug *(or did he?)*. He jumped up, grabbed one of my big toes in his mouth and hung on to it. It was a BOOM/FLASH/GRAB all at once and it was my knee-jerk response that lifted the stone table. If that ain't frog humor, then what is?

When I was courting Kathy, aside from teaching her to catch night crawlers (the big earthworms) with a flashlight, we'd go out riding around on the back roads at night during a spring thunderstorm. All these hundreds of toads would come out on the pavement and so many of them got smashed under car tires. We'd take turns driving and jumping out to grab toads. We'd fill 5-gallon buckets a quarter full with toads of all sizes. Then we'd bring them up home and release them in the gardens. What a way to win a woman's heart! I mean how romantic can you get!

I often bring groups of children down to tour the sunroom

and ask them, "Do you smell anything foul or pukey?" They say, "No it's nice down here." That's especially true when the jasmine is in bloom. Then I take them back to the recycling shed and ask them the same question and I get the same answer. Then I ask, "When you lift up the cover of a dumpster what do you smell?" I hear, "Eww, yuck, gross!" Then I tell them, "The same thing that's in the dumpster is divided between the sunroom and the recycling shed." I had one kid start running around yelling, "There's no such thing as garbage up here!

I don't burn synthetic or organic materials just to be rid of them. I either process or compost. With one exception: I've saved all the empty aerosol cans generated over the years because I've reasoned that the best way to deal with them and the residue inside them is with a huge, hellacious, once-in-a-lifetime bonfire. It'll be Ted's big contribution to the greenhouse effect. I may just do it one of these days. First I'll remove all the plastic spray nozzles and when the big party fire is at its the hottest point, I'll toss all the cans into the center at once and run like hell. It'll be my own personal fireworks display. Maybe I'll get a keg and invite some friends. Who knows? Maybe one of those steel balls you hear when you're shaking the paint can will hit me in the back like a musket ball. Maybe I'll deserve it.

Landfills and Garbage

For many years I claimed that I never sent anything to the landfill. However, once I became so overwhelmed by the futility of my practice that I sank into a state of deep despair. In that depressed state I sent to the landfill all my worn out shoes,

30-plus years of empty caulking tubes and a double-lined stainless steel stove pipe filled with asbestos dust that had ruptured and was spilling out. I basically lost the virginity of my practice.

I only disposed of the equivalent of what I'd seen some affluent (or should I say effluent) families set out for the garbage collector in a week. It was my 30 years to their single week. Had I kept the faith, I could have maintained my virginity. I'm sorry I lost it. I could have dealt with that stuff. I could have rinsed out that asbestos dust and mixed it in some concrete pour and then hauled the stainless to the scrap yard. I just felt so damned defeated. I basically "What's the point-ed" myself into a corner.

Waste has been with us throughout our evolution. It was okay to just toss stuff out with no concern in our primitive years because everything we used was organic and compostable. That meant its stain on the landscape washed out with water. It's the synthetic stains that don't wash out that depress the hell out of me.

What is organic has a place in the big organism (the ecosphere). Organic means nature will assimilate and transform it. Then we started inventing synthetic alternatives to replace organic substances because there weren't enough willow trees to make all the aspirin we needed. The trouble is, there's no place in the ecosphere for synthetics. They have nowhere to go because nature is hard pressed to assimilate and transform them. They appear to dissipate but then they re-concentrate, maybe in your liver or in the fish that you and the bald eagle just had for dinner. Even when we "productively" harness synthetics to quick-fix things like those enormous blemish-free, uniform apples, it's really no more than sorcery with side effects.

So who was the first asshole that justified his individual right to throw or pour some synthesized nightmare into the stream of life that didn't belong there? All I wanted to be was the first asshole that did his best not to. Tossing out crap that isn't biodegradable as if you're getting rid of it? Come on now! Einstein said the idea we can cast something away for good is pure illusion. Now if we don't see we're being taught that lesson every day then it's quite possible we have our heads tucked up somewhere they don't belong. All that stuff we think we're getting rid of is ending up in the food chain and from there it enters our organs, our bloodstream and our newborn infants.

But still for some reason people seem to have the impulse to dump shit and old carcasses in the stream, even when they have the option to drag it off into the forest and compost it properly and productively. I really do think that an original transgression is at the bottom of it all, an original disobedience, think what you will. We're not all bad though. We have a good side as well. I have the greatest faith that we will arise like a phoenix out of the ashes of our demise. I can see it happening already.

My Affair with the Landfill

When my wife and I ate out at Taco Bell, or anywhere for that matter, we used to bring home our trash and absorb it into our recycling system. Because of that same sense of overwhelming futility that seduced me to have intercourse with the landfill, we eventually quit bringing home our Taco Bell trash. I have a feeling we may resume the practice one day, maybe not. If some of you'd be willing to do it too, I'd surely start again. I just don't want to be the only one. I need support. Maybe we could start a club or something.

It wasn't just a sense of futility that drove me to those changes in behavior. I also had a sort of half-assed justification brewing in my brain. I really believe the landfill will one day be mined for resource just like we mine minerals. It's been said that 1/3 of the world's copper is still in the ground, 1/3 is in our wires and plumbing, and 1/3 is in the landfill. I just hope when the time comes we do it right and complete. If we don't entirely take the concept of garbage out of the landfill we'll just make another mess for our grandkids to deal with.

I attended a lecture presented at a local college titled "The Myth of Recycling." It was all about how recycling is a waste of time and energy. Knee-high rubber boots weren't enough to cut through that sloppy, verbose b.s. You needed hip waders, the kind fishermen use that go up to your chest. I have to ask: Can a supposedly highly educated person have the insight and clarity to speak about the importance of recycling while at the same time having an affair with his garbage can? I think it would be like trusting advice about fidelity from some guy whose sexing his best friend's wife.

You can't possibly derive from classroom speculation about what I've come to realize in 35 years of pondering and agonizing over my actual living practice 24/7. Of course when you're getting a paycheck to say that kind of stuff, what can you expect? A fact here, a fact there and presto, you've dressed up your sick political-ideological fantasy in sexy lingerie.

I realize opinions are likely to form in the absence of facts.

So you might say the same of me and my opinions, but I'm not having an ongoing affair with a garbage can and to this day I've scarcely made a cent for saying what I'm saying. My words come from personal conviction. Yes, I fell and had an affair with the landfill, but that just gave me more pause to reflect on my marriage. And when you think about it, I'd trust advice about fidelity more from a guy who had it, lost it and then regained it again. He knows every implication about fidelity because he experienced it from all angles. So now I'll tell you straight out what my perspective is and I'll weigh it against "The Myth of Recycling" any day of the week.

More problems arise from the concept of "garbage" than we can ever even imagine. I'm talking disease, cancer, addiction, neurosis, depression and especially the ever-widening gap between the rich and poor. I'll go so far as to say that at the very least, a large portion of society's ills can and will be traced directly to living a disposable mentality. I view disposability as just one of the big three primary causes of hell on earth that we can actually do something about. The other two are fossil fuels and unbridled snake oil salesmanship.

The Broken Circle

What we see as waste was the very thing that was meant to circle around to feed and renew the earth's vitality. Most of us have heard of the food chain, natural law, survival of the fittest and "the circle of life." These are thought bites for how the mechanics actually work. The food chain describes how more simple life forms link to sustain more complex ones on up till you get to man. We're just starting to understand the circle of life because we're still mentally hamstrung by linear thought. We're still inclined to think the circle into a long straight line with two distinct ends.

Linear thought is the curse that severs extreme opposites like dominion and stewardship and places them at opposite ends. It forbids the first to touch the last, the greatest to touch the least, by separating them with an unbridgeable gulf. Without that touch they cannot achieve the contradiction that links the line into a circle. We, humankind, are that contradiction.

I had a second cousin, Russell. He was a huge, gigantic "Rain Man." He could tell you how many seconds you've lived, when a Roadway truck was about to come down the mountain and that a plane was gonna fly from the west in three minutes. He'd pick us up high in the air, tickle the hell out of us, then squeeze us hard and scare us shitless.

I heard that when they first came out with an adding machine at the post office, they let Russell glance at a page in the phonebook. He added all the numbers in a few seconds and rattled off a total. Then he gave it back to the postal clerk with the adding machine. I don't know exactly how long it took the clerk to add the numbers, but it was way, way longer than Russell's two-second glance. The clerk punched in the last number and pushed the sum button and their numbers didn't correspond. Simple, childlike Russell said, "You're wrong, do it again." They found out later that Russell's sum was correct.

The thing about Russell was that you couldn't look at his being an idiot of sorts without it instantly being cancelled by his genius, and vice-versa. They were both so powerfully manifest in him. If you thought of him as an idiot his genius would roar up and pounce on that thought like a lion. Russell was the point of contradiction where opposites link. You literally couldn't say or even think him to be one or the other. That's the very way I believe our dominion and our stewardship are supposed to relate. Look at the war that linear thinking has created by imagining the two into far left and far right. Now you've got Greenpeace on one side and "drill baby drill" on the other.

Our dominion and our stewardship should really be wishing to be wed within each of us. It's their marriage that brings peace and it's the only way to heal the neurosis that arises from their divorce status. Their union makes dominion and stewardship one thing, and the two becoming one is what reconnects the circle of life.

The life of the Native American completely revolved around necessity. Waste and ecological narcissism were a shock to their perception, their spiritual belief and their lifestyle. I repeat the words of my distant ancestors who, upon first witnessing the me-my-mine exploiting mindset of the white settlers, said to themselves, "Now the great circle is broken."

These days we're slowly coming to see that everything actually is linked and interdependent. Often by hard lessons, we're learning that a single disturbance in a single link eventually resonates throughout all the other links. We are slowly realizing that life forms are meant to coexist in a state of mutual benefit and that sustainability is a two-way street as opposed to a one-way boulevard leading directly to man just because the Bible is interpreted to say that we have King James' "dominion."

A good example of how the two-way street works in the circle of life is the food chain link between the wolf and the caribou. The fastest strongest and cleverest of the wolf pack can only cull and feed upon the weakest and slowest of the caribou herd. The strength and preservation of the wolf species are fed and sustained. In this magic, what is erased from both the pack and the herds are their defects, weaknesses, the old and the injured. What is preserved in both is their strength and vitality. We can easily predict what might happen were either the wolf or the caribou suddenly given the power to reason. They'd just do what we do. They'd find a way to transgress natural law. The wolf would reason ways to feast on the strongest caribou's sweet and tender vitality or the caribou would reason ways to completely evade the wolf. Either way it would be a great disturbance that would send shock waves throughout the circle of life. And it might mean eventual extinction for both.

If we think the earth's majesty was made just for us, that it's ours to harvest at a whim, we've been fooled into believing a dominion-based lie. A prophet somewhere in the apocryphal writings said there is one ordinance, one law, one way that creation works, and that man can't see it for his arrogance. He didn't say the ordinance is hidden, or that it's complicated or above our ability to comprehend, he said it's because we're arrogant.

The Paradigm of Necessity

During the Second World War, what was this entire nation doing to "support our troops" and address the common threat? It was recycling – down to the gum wrapper. Now we are fighting more hidden threats than we even care to imagine or admit, and what do we base our economy on? Planned obsolescence, non-renewable resources and consumer waste.

Our exploitation of creation is the exploitation of our very own spirit. In giving we receive, in the sacrificial act of enriching the needy, we ourselves are enriched. Doesn't it stand to reason that we are both healed and fulfilled in the selfless act of enriching creation's majesty, and made poorer in our exploitation of it?

The paradigm of desire is over. The paradigm of necessity is here. It's to turn out the lights when you leave the room. It's to slice open your toothpaste tube so none goes to waste. It's to subsist on a diet of carefully washed out plastic zip bags so you never in your life have to buy a new box of them. It's to buy all your dress and work clothes at the G.W. Boutique (Goodwill Store) while supporting the economy in the purchase of new underclothes and bath towels.

It Doesn't Have To Be This Way

The landfill is but a great heap of uniquely cultured Petri dishes. What do environmental scientists fear most? "The Petri dish effect" of every sealed plastic mayonnaise and catsup bottle cultured with a mixture of virus and bacteria from each house it came from. Plastic and other synthetics that end up in the oceans and waterways create their own hellish consequences. The greatest of the three known plastic vortexes in the Pacific Ocean is said to be the size of Rhode Island. There's plastic in it from the time DuPont invented it. It has now permeated the flesh of some marine life and has become a feared biohazard. A chunk of it is said to have broken free and is drifting toward the shore of the Antarctic and is about too unleash its infectious nightmare.

Albatrosses are found starved to death because their stomachs are filled with Bic lighters, synthetic wine corks and every imaginable floating piece of plastic trash. Turtles are mistaking plastic bags for the jellyfish they feed on. The atrocities are endless. Plastic should be controlled just two degrees shy of nuclear waste. It has proper applications, but in the disposable role it just stinks.

Disposability creates a myriad disasters waiting to happen and we wonder why there's so much chaos and disease. The landfill simply should not and does not have to exist. Industry created it so industry should abolish it. Take tires, for just one example: You've probably seen images of those mountains of discarded tires that have been burning for years, spewing pollution and just about impossible to extinguish. Abandoned tires are everywhere we look, tossed into rivers and streams across the land. Aside from the insult to the environment, those tires are breeding grounds for disease-bearing mosquitoes. If for some reason you had to actually design an ultimate mosquito breeder you'd be hard pressed to do better than an abandoned tire. It's solar heated and it's an unsurpassed water catch system that a mosquito could hover in during high winds. We have West Nile virus and are about to face Dengue fever moving up from the south. Abandoned tires are everywhere. When you do the math, it's a pretty scary picture.

So who should be responsible for this? Is it really us who pay 200 bucks for 3/8-inch of wear, or is it Goodrich, Uniroyal, Firestone and Michelin? Appliances, vehicles, furniture, carpets, plastic wrap, cigarette butts and on and on – I only pay for the use of them. Who then is responsible for their abandoned cores and carcasses? I'd say the ones who manufactured them. Industry itself is responsible because industry alone profits from their abandonment. But I am seeing a couple of signs of progress, with people finding ways to shred old tires and use them for road paving and other applications. It's a start. Technologies from Asia are showing us ways to extract usable oil from tires. New industries are getting the idea that it's a win-win proposition to jump on the recycling bandwagon.

You can help speed up the process of making landfills a thing of the past by raising your voice, writing your elected public officials. Ask them what good are recycling labels on things if there's no easy avenue, or no avenue whatsoever, to recycle them. Take just a tiny step toward necessity today, any step, and then find another to take tomorrow.

And while you're at it, get to know your local frogs, snakes and night crawlers. They're working for you.

7

TURNING HOUSEHOLD PLASTICS INTO BUILDING BLOCKS

(kind of like swords into plowshares)

*"...a logical and very practical new beginning for
plastic wrap's ending is as a multi-purpose building block."*

tip

Now, down to the practical aspects of recycling, starting with household plastics. There are two bulk materials we amass that are not easy to recycle back into the system. One is Styrofoam (cups, trays and packing). We feed our Styrofoam into a garden chipper and use it for insulation. The other thing that nature has a hard time absorbing is plastic wrap and bags, the stuff we use every day that's so much a part of our lives it's near to invisible.

I've said that it's important to wash and thoroughly dry plastic wrap and other "garbage" before it's re-used or sorted and stored for later use. At our house there is almost always some amount of it to wash with every cycle of dishes. We do our dishes by hand. Washing plastic wrap and other recyclables takes about a quarter or less of the entire dish washing effort. Above the kitchen sink we have a couple of sharp, multi-pronged hooks that we impale the plastic on as we wash (another of our improvised but very useful tools). Then we hang it near the wood stove to dry in the winter or just air-dry it in the summer.

After we'd been doing this for a while we couldn't help noticing that we had accumulated a huge amount of plastic wrap that we didn't have any practical use for. It certainly wasn't going to go into some landfill. We'd been saving all our Friendship Farms bread bags and stuffing them like sausages with all that dry, miscellaneous plastic wrap, and tying the ends shut. Not everything went into the bags. I have a use for what I call "squishy plastic," which I keep separate because of its lifelike property: You can squish it into a ball and watch it slowly expand. I've used it to seal off large air leaks. I also store separately any plastic wrap that has a reflective surface.

But what about all those bread bags stuffed with plastic wrap? Kathy and I brainstormed a lot of ideas about what to do with it before we hit on this, "the cat's ass" of all my inventions: compressed plastic building blocks.

We had two compactors up here at the house, and an extra one stored in the big warehouse down at my dad's. I had bought one for us at the flea market, was given another unit, and then started seeing lots of them at yard sales. People don't use them much nowadays, so they're cheap, going for about $15. If you get one, make sure you also buy a lifetime supply of insert bags.

Just last weekend we reconfigured our entire recycling

system. We installed one compactor permanently in the recycling shed, which has now become the processing shed. Now all the recycling is done here in the main house. The categories are sorted and stored to volume in one room. To have the main house deal with both organic and synthetic is a big change that we'd contemplated for a long time. My buddy Cal suggested it.

But back to our experiment with that first compressed plastic building block. It's unbelievably deceiving how much will fill a block. I remember Kathy looking at our collection of clothes-lined plastic wrap, saying, "This should make at least three full blocks." That turned out to be wishful thinking. It barely made one.

The first time, I start tossing the stuffed Friendship Farms bread bags into the compactor, closing the drawer and pushing the button. I did it again and again until it couldn't take any more, then I pulled the compacted block out and wrapped it tight with duct tape. I found that in my Sears compactor one year's worth of plastic wrap compacted into a single block.

Now that I had my first block, I needed to finish it in a way that made it into something useful to people. For my immediate needs I'm putting my blocks into the icehouse walls for highly efficient insulation. But a logical and very practical new beginning for plastic wrap's ending is as a multi-purpose building block. If you're interested in this concept, I've described its design and uses below. This is for an exterior building block. The ones I have on stock will be used in my icehouse. They will not have the finish described below, nor will they be encased in reflective material.

What you'll need:
- A garbage/trash compactor
- Galvanized lath screen (comes in 32" by 8' sheets)
- Sand
- Portland cement
- (Optional) Any wrapping material that has reflective properties: potato chip bags, candy wrappers, miscellaneous Mylar, bonded aluminum foil, etc. Pure aluminum foil should be taken to the scrap yard and reintroduced into the system, although you won't be paid much for it.
- (Optional) Locksmith dust or any brass or copper filings.

The prototype I made first is 14" x 22" x 22" inches. The actual compacted block is about 3" less in each dimension, because there's a 1½" gap between the block and the lath screen cage, which is bent by hand and formed to contain it. To bend the lath screen you can do it freehand or form it over the edge of something. I used the edge of a porch deck.

The gap on all sides is stuffed with the loose, reflective material. That's a very simple to do. Just put a good amount of it in the bottom of the lath screen box, insert and center the compacted block into the screen cage, and then pack all sides including the top. Then close the lid of your lath screen box and wire it shut.

Now mix only enough cement to do one side (the bottom), using one part Portland cement to 3 or 4 parts sand. Then carefully add water and mix until you have a nice working consistency. It has to stick but not run off or sag. The lath screen is designed to grab the wet cement and hold it. Then trowel it onto the lath and let it set up (dry). If you have a little extra cement just use it up by starting to work up the side, but don't try to do it all at once. Once it's dry, flip it over, so the side you did first becomes the bottom, and then proceed to do the other four sides and the top.

I dusted the sides with locksmith dust while they were still wet. As it oxidizes it gives a nice bluish-green patina to the block. You also have the option to seal the whole block with some sort of water seal for concrete, but give it a year to patina before you do if you want that kind of finish.

Now that you have a block, what can you do with it?

Three Practical Uses

Super-insulators

My personal stock of "plastic bales" is slated for use in my double-walled icehouse. The compacted blocks will be strategically set amidst chipped-up Styrofoam between the walls. As they're inserted, their duct tape binding will be cut on one side so they slowly expand and compact the Styrofoam. Of course I have to make sure I seal the cap of the double wall as soon as it's filled. If I don't, it'll all come out like a slow motion volcano. For a description of the icehouse construction, see the Refrigeration chapter.

Interlocked walls

You can use them as a high wall that needs a good bit of downward or sideward sheer strength. The diagram on p. 97 shows

*Preparing the lath screen box to receive a compacted
and wrapped plastic block.*

*Surrounding the block with reflective material
and applying cement*

Finished prototype block

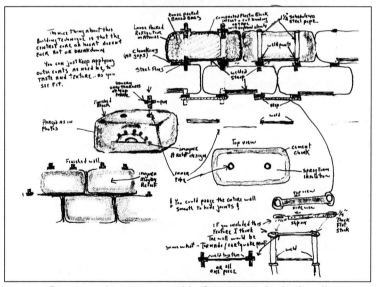

**Diagram showing assembly for an interlocked wall
of compacted plastic blocks.
For a larger image visit www.thestonecamp.com.**

how to interlock them for lightweight or heavyweight sheer strength, similar to the way scaffolding is stacked up the side of high buildings (for a larger image, visit www.thestonecamp.com). The lightweight version can use the same gauge of thinner wall pipe that scaffolding has. If you want to go up many stories and be hurricane-proof, I'd use something like the heavy Schedule 40 pipe in the picture.

What I like about this idea is its resistance to internal or structural entropy. The only thing that might deteriorate is the apparent external stucco finish. That can be redone over and over and over with no side effects other than your wall gains a bit of thickness. You could even recoat the surface with a new layer of lath screen sheeting and gain nothing but thickness and strength. There are many commercial brands of stucco material that have polymers and sealants in the mixture.

"Straw bale" construction

Another option for these compacted blocks is a building procedure that is the same as the straw bale construction technique. This technique of building involves stacking the blocks (the same as with straw bales) loosely into the wall dimension you desire, then covering the whole wall face with the same lath screen and then plaster or stucco it with the same cement mixture.

I'm surely not knocking straw bale construction. I'd be really tempted to build a house with straw, except for the fact the little piggy who did the same got his house huffed, puffed and blown down. Just kidding. I'd love to build a straw bale house. All I'd like to say is that plastic blocks are superior to straw bales in many ways. First off, you know for sure that plastic bales are never going to decompose or dry rot. The second thing is that it's using up what is clogging the landfills, the oceans and the world, for that matter. It's an excellent beginning to the end of disposable plastic wrap.

Plastic blocks also mimic two ecological principles in two ways that straw bale construction doesn't. Plastic is a fossil fuel. It's made from oil. Nature's first concern is that fossil fuels are buffered from the biosphere. That buffer increases with time, and nothing in life has a natural appetite for it. The incomplete decomposition of fossil fuels to inert beyond putridity is simply toxic to life's digestive system.

So these plastic building blocks accomplish two things: #1, they mimic nature's buffer, and #2, they take a landfill end and give it a new beginning. Straw, on the other hand, is bio-degradable. It wants to be eaten and the biosphere drools for it. It seems better composted into a soil amendment. To stick it in a wall goes against nature because it stops a process that nature intended for it. Logic seems to whisper, "Keep the pet-rochemicals out of the field and put the organic amendments on them instead."

You might feel compelled to counter with the argument, "Well, what about using wood? It's like straw in a way, isn't it?" I'm not pro or con, I'm only stating a few facts. I build with wood, I run the family's sawmill, and I think straw bale is really cool. But a compressed plastic block? Now that's something I can truly feel good about using.

Here's a thought for the future: What if, in real estate, super-insulated walls and foundation were constructed in such a way that it would be pointless and redundant to tear them down in order to rebuild? I'm picturing a fast food place going out of business and another business buying the building – but instead of razing the whole thing, they strip it to its base walls and foundation and then reface it into a Taco Bell, say. What if all art and creativity was expressed in the re-faced finish of the walls and the roof? What if you bought real estate for existing square footage and location alone? Then what you bought would be your 3-D canvas to re-face and decorate – a canvas of the walls I've just described. If the walls were my LEGO-like plastic building blocks, think how easily additions could be assembled and then textured to taste. I'm not expecting Taco Bell to call me anytime soon.

It's Not Just About Plastic Blocks

I'd like you to view our lifestyle itself as a prototype practice. If we're to re-gear our economy under an "end-to-beginning" parameter, everybody is going to have to do their part and work together with industry. In other words, if industry is to ever succeed in becoming responsible for their endeavors, we have to prepare ourselves and change our own behavior. We have to be willing to help them out and work with them so we all do what's right.

Compared to what's possible to develop, what I do is crude and labor intensive. We're looking for the most streamline user-friendly system that is somewhere between unfriendly and intolerant of those who don't follow and participate in it. You just can't search out every litterbug and beat the shit out of him, because there will always be another to take his place. We need to make it benefit the litterbug not to litter.

The shift will happen, but it must be profitable for everyone to participate. And then you'll see changes too numerous to count. You'll see the gap between rich and poor diminish, the fog of psychological depression and dysfunction begin to lift, bigotry become more transparent, and beautification bloom in the public landscapes. If and when we perfect our economy with ecological principles, it will be like waking up from a nightmare. If I can take a flea market compactor and a pile of cast-off plastic wrap and make something useful and pleasing to Mother Nature, imagine what other creative solutions are out there just waiting to be taken up and worked with.

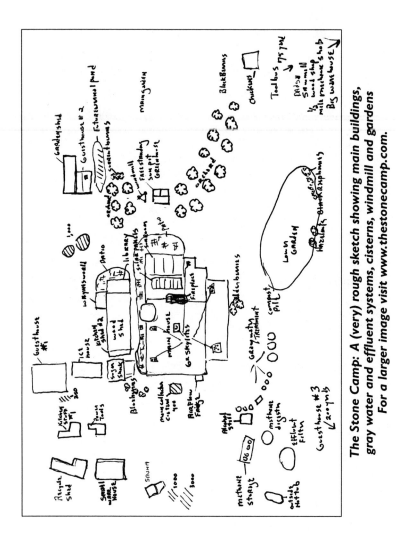

The Stone Camp: *A (very) rough sketch showing main buildings, gray water and effluent systems, cisterns, windmill and gardens For a larger image visit www.thestonecamp.com.*

PART TWO

The Systems

All life is an experiment.
The more experiments you make the better.

– RALPH WALDO EMERSON

Southern exposure – welcoming the sunlight

8

At Home

"We first had to put in place a series of highly efficient, functional and often wildly inventive systems."

⌀℘

From the time it was first built, The Stone Camp seems to have always had a life and fate of its own, and I seem to have been sent to the best college of experience and hard knocks to become its CEO. Basically, once upon a time, long, long ago, somebody was moved to build a place too far out in the boonies to get a power line to it. Then one day Peter Pan moved in, called up all the lost boys and girls he knew and they made it into their Never-Never Land.

I took over at the point of its rebirth and parented it through childhood, adolescence and early adulthood, with Kathy by my side for much of it. Now the tables are about to turn. As we have tended it, we expect that it will tend to us now. They say that parents fully mature back into children, and one day the parent must be tended by the child. The Stone Camp is our child.

Kathy will retire in a few years. By that time we hope the growth spurts will have stopped and we'll be able to slip into a kind of monastic maintenance lifestyle. (That's a big hope. I'll have to give up caffeine and exorcize that work ethic demon that's been whipping my ass all these years.) The most amazing thing – something we comment on a lot – is how much easier things seem to get, year after year. Tapping trees, cutting firewood, prepping the garden...every year feels like less and less work.

We didn't get to this point all at once, as you know by now. We first had to put in place a series of highly efficient, functional and often wildly inventive systems. I'll start with the sunroom, which could also be called the greenhouse, but it's so much more then either of those names.

The Sunroom

If The Stone Camp is a kind of conscious entity, as I truly believe, then the sunroom comprises some of its most important organs. People ask where I came up with the idea to build it. Did I draw up plans? Did I read about one in a book? And where did I get the idea to bring the water from the rain gutter through the wall to water the earth inside? I say "No" to the first question, "Maybe, I can't remember" to the second, and "From nowhere" to the third. The sunroom built itself. It all happened spontaneously. I don't expect you'll rush out and build your own sunroom the way mine got itself built.

It started when my dog Beowulf died. I was devastated. I could hardly walk for mourning and weeping. He had been half of me for 16 years, since before Kathy was living here. When Beowulf died I brought Dad's backhoe up to dig the grave a little beyond the house. I was actually puking from grief as I laid Wulfie to rest.

After I pushed the dirt back in and covered the grave I turned the machine around and headed back down to Dad's place. I only got about 30 yards when I stopped by the door of the house that faced south, no doubt because I was crying too hard to drive any farther. But I didn't get off the machine and shut it down. I just sat there on the seat for a moment. Then all of a sudden I backed the machine up to that south-facing door, set the outriggers and started digging. And I kept on digging. There was a voice of rationale saying (yelling), "Ted, stop, you don't know what you're doing. Look, you're making a big mess, stop!" I could barely even think because I was locked into venting my emotions through the backhoe levers. Next thing you know there's a huge hole beside my house about the size of the one Wulfie's death just left in my soul.

All that had been in my mind was an un-germinated un-manifest cosmic seed of a sunroom. The merest inkling. Maybe I saw a picture of one and thought about it over a coffee buzz, I really don't remember, but that's how the sunroom happened: no plans, no vivid imagery, just a microscopic seed that got so flooded by the moisture of tears that it germinated and came to life. Next thing I knew, the heavy mourning subsided and I was hiking along railroad tracks looking for big granite cobblestones to edge the sunroom's terraces and encase the hot tub/shower stall.

As you come into our house today and look across the entry room you'll glimpse the sunroom. You're looking down into a living jungle. In deep winter it offers a Shangri-la, lost world kind of contrast to the snow and ice outside. When we've got the hammock hung, it could be Tarzan's bedroom. Stand at the entrance to the sunroom and you're looking down at five terraced levels descending to the bottom floor, with steps down the middle. Each tier is like a huge, odd-shaped planter. Each is walled on all sides and filled with earth, but the first three tiers have no bottom. They go straight to mother earth. Grab a shovel and they become doors to China.

For the past 20 or more years we have buried all of our kitchen compost in that terraced earth, except for citrus peels. There are great unseen colonies of red worms that migrate toward and from the buried kitchen waste. They'll consume two gallons in four weeks and produce one of the finest organic fertilizers known to man: worm castings. We pack a woman's stocking with the worm castings and suspend it in a 55-gallon drum of water for a few days, then we spray it on the garden (for foliage, we dilute it again to 10 to 1 with water).

The interior dimensions of the sunroom are 13' 9" x 12' 7". It's set 3½ feet below outside ground level. The below-ground-level walls, along with half the floor space of the sunroom, act like a French-drained thermos bottle. There's even a 2-inch layer of Styrofoam under the concrete floor. The inner walls are stucco-ed concrete block, filled with vermiculite and chipped Styrofoam for insulation. Every so often I fill a vertical column of aligned hollows in the block with wet, runny concrete mix and hammer a section of rebar down through it to keep the walls from bulging inward.

I painted the outside of the block with a tar-based foundation paint, then wrapped it in a layer of Slater's roofing felt paper. I added two inches of Styrofoam to the outside of that and wrapped the whole thing in a layer of heavy mil plastic. Then I backfilled the foundation.

The roof is all glass, four stripped-out sliding glass doors set and sealed in 6 x 6 Wolmanized beams at a 30-degree slant for optimum winter sun harvest. Aside from the 3½-foot-high block walls, most of the remaining wall space in the sunroom is taken up by a large picture window. One wall in the hot tub/shower is stone and the other is slated with roof slate.

The most important step in finishing out the sunroom was waiting for frigid outdoor temperature so I could test for air leaks. I got the main wood stove burning real hot, using a lot of air, then dipped my hands in water and went all around the inside walls to feel for air leaks. Doing that, you can literally find them blindfolded.

By the time I was done, I had about $350 in the whole project. It so much built itself that I strain to even remember laboring on it. All I can tell you is there used to be a conventional south wall to the house, with the usual windows, and now that has been replaced by a complete environment that is hard to adequately describe without your being here to see it. It's so multifaceted and multi-functional, I'm constantly amazed by what it does. Just sitting down there is a joy.

Glimpsing the sunroom from the entry room

*Some of the earthen terraced levels of the sunroom,
our living jungle*

*Exterior of sunroom, showing solar panels and
recycled sliding glass doors*

The sunroom's hot tub/shower

The sunroom is an organ that not only has to do with digesting kitchen scraps to provide nutrition, it's also a womb that gives birth to all the garden plants in February and March and nourishes them till they go outside into the ground. The coolest thing is it acts as the lungs of the house. There is a constant flow pattern to the house air that sends and cycles it through its living plants.

There's great depth and mystery and many hidden things and life forms here: whole shelves of beautiful knickknacks, carved seals, huge crystals, an abalone shell filled with beautiful shapes and marbles, all lost and forgotten, consumed within a ravenous jasmine plant and an avocado tree that got out of hand. The jasmine blooms in January and fills the house with a sweet aroma at the same time as we're bringing in the rough-boiled maple sap to the 5-gallon stainless steel finishing pot on the main wood heating stove in the kitchen nearby. It's a month of breathing and tasting sweetness. We're constantly using "the sippy cup" to sample maple syrup to perfection with jasmine pouring in our nostrils.

The whole room is also a passive solar heater that absorbs and stores heat in the granite stones and flagstone floors. Then it slowly releases the heat after the sun goes down. I've gone down there late at night, barefoot in winter, and after a cold but sunny day the stones will be warm. The sunroom is also a hotel for our staff of sentient life forms. The frogs and toads that live in there hop through the house at night. They hunt down and consume harmful insects, like white blood cells hunting down a bacterial infection.

In the winter we grow wheat grass here for juicing. I believe wheat grass is one of the most therapeutic things we could enjoy. In that sense the sunroom functions as an immune system booster. This year we found we can grow kale and celery here. One of these winters we hope to experiment with a few other edible greens, some cherry tomatoes and maybe some green beans and cucumbers. Just another facet of the sunroom's nutrition system.

Right now I already have 30 irons in 30 fires, but ultimately I do hope to get into growing exotic fruits – figs, lemons, limes, oranges and maybe a dwarf banana or two. I'll be keeping them in the sunroom over winter.

The Sunroom's Hot Tub

There's a small claw foot bathtub to the right as you walk down the terraced steps. It's encased in granite and has flagstone around the top. It doubles as a hot tub and shower stall. On the lowest tier of the room, the left half is earth and the right half has a flagstone floor with a huge stone table and two chairs. There's a separate little wood stove down there, too. Its hot chimney exhaust flows directly under the length of the tub, through the western wall and then up its own chimney. It operates similar to how the Romans heated their floors and public baths.

There's even a sand-based pool filter and 12-volt Jacuzzi pump for the tub, to give you more options. I remember one evening sitting in it, long before the picture window became completely consumed by the jungle of jasmine and a composted avocado seed that decided to grow. I'm sipping on a glass of wine and my eyes are shifting back and forth from 17 deer outside to a Star Trek episode on the old 5-inch black and white TV. I remember that was the year of watching deer. I could see as much difference from one to another as I could see in people. There was one elegant Cleopatra-like doe I called The Princess.

Instead of a solid curtain, the tub is now hidden behind seemingly infinite hanging pieces of natural beauty. It's wonderful to take visiting infants down there and watch their eyes as they look around at the light and color, some of it coming through an old stained-glass window that Ruth Scott gave me, which is suspended from the ceiling by two chains.

We don't use it as a hot tub much anymore because we have the one outside that Kathy and I can both fit into. But we have speculated that the one in the sunroom would function very much like one of those huge Russian wood heaters, the kind you fire once real hot every few days with sticks and stuff, and it stays hot. Not much of the heat is lost because the hot exhaust from the fire has to travel through such a long maze of flue channels. That causes most of the heat from the quick fire to be absorbed in the huge mass of stone, brick and mortar. Once absorbed, it slowly releases the heat into the house and keeps you warm for days.

We thought that if we ever had to leave for a couple of days in winter we'd heat the tub full of water, really hot, which would also heat the mass of stone and mortar that surround it. Then if we laid the thin backpacker's sleeping mat that we use, like a lid, to insulate the water on top while it's heating, it would most likely store and slowly dissipate the heat into the house for days. That would be nice to come home to.

Hot Water

You might be wondering about our hot water source for the tub and shower.

We have two ways to heat utility water, one for each of the two showers in the house. For a long time, the hot water for our bathroom shower was fed exclusively from the wood stove hot water system, and the greenhouse shower was fed only from the solar hot water system, and wasn't used in winter for obvious reasons. They are both convection-heating systems that require no pumps, which means they employ the principle of heat rising and cold sinking. The hot water rises (flows) to the storage tank that is positioned higher than the heat source, and the cold water sinks (flows) back down to contact the heat source. The heated water always has some place to go.

If your solar water heater is on the roof and your storage tank is in the basement, you have to force it down with pumps because there's no "up there" place for the heat to go. If you didn't forcefully pump the hot water down, it would just expand, perhaps boil and build pressure. With nowhere to go, it would be like firing up a steam locomotive but not releasing the steam to drive the wheels. Something would explode or pop, hopefully just your pressure release valve and not your expensive solar hot water panel.

In a convection system such as mine there's a formula dealing with the height and the horizontal distance your storage tank is away from the stove. It's in a book I have/had that somebody borrowed, "Handmade Hot Water Systems." Please return it, whoever you are.

I got so attached to showering in our sunroom/greenhouse I wanted to use it all year instead of just in the summer. In the winter it's like you're showering under a waterfall in a steamy jungle while just outside the window it's a bleak winter wonderland. To make the sunroom shower use either summer solar or winter wood hot water meant I had to make some major changes in the plumbing system. I figured it would take maybe three ½-inch valves and I gave myself three hours to do it. Well, that turned into another "Ted, what the hell are you doing" event. Thirteen ½-inch valves and three days later my voice was hoarse from endless profanities. That was a labor I do remember laboring over, probably because it was desire based. It just wasn't necessary.

9

FOOD AND OUR
KITCHEN LIFESTYLE

"We envisioned an Eden of fruits and vegetables."

✐

Here at The Stone Camp, everything is connected to everything else. Indoors and outdoors merge into a continual flow of life. Our kitchen is the center of life. It brings it all together, being the place where we cook, prepare and process food, finish maple syrup in the winter and do many other things that make our lives comfortable and enjoyable. But I first want to take you outside to the garden, to see the soil.

Soil

I'm not exaggerating when I say that the soil represents our very being, and that the disease of our culture may be symptomatic of the disease of the soil. They are perfect mirrors of each other. Everything from the Dust Bowl to the depletion of life force via petrochemical dependence is suffered in us directly and indirectly. And conversely, in the healing, organic enrichment and stability of the soil we ourselves are healed and stabilized. In the soil we touch our organic root. That touch itself is our health and sanity. I believe that the healing of our ecosystem, any aspect of it, from forests to waterways, begins in the soil.

One of the first things Kathy and I did was plan a garden. We envisioned an Eden of fruits and vegetables. But getting there was another thing. The best sun was on the south side of the house where there was an old 4,000 square foot dry lakebed, a place that caught the most sun. It looked like a giant, empty mud puddle that would be three or four feet deep if it was full. All it needed was to be filled with topsoil, lots of it. I brought up a big International bulldozer and excavated the lakebed in preparation. There's an old farm on one of the first foothills of the Laurel Ridge where a distant cousin lives with his wife. In exchange for coming in with my D4 Caterpillar to improve the grade on his property, I skimmed off 14 dump truck loads of his topsoil. It came from land on either side of a small steam that feeds his lake. It was good, black, rich earth that had eroded out of the forest on land that hadn't been farmed for generations.

It wasn't enough to fill our lakebed, so I ordered an additional 35 tons delivered. Not long after that I met my buddy Scott who worked at a horse farm and we were given unlimited truckloads of an extremely old, extremely composted mixture of horse manure and sawdust. It was the most wonderful stuff with a rich, pure, earthy smell. You'd never have guessed what it was. I worked layer upon layer of it into the topsoil.

In some places the topsoil in the old lakebed is three feet

deep. Now, it takes nature 1,000 years to create one inch of top-soil. I estimate that what we have is a good 36,000 years' worth. I once stood overlooking the garden with one of the richest men in this area of the country (he actually came up my driveway in a stretch limo)… I said, "Benny, this dirt is my stock portfolio, my 401K. If I leave this place that soil goes with me." He got a kick out of that.

As I look around at this garden and the lower garden, I'm thinking we could start to catch up on things if I could clone 20 Teddies. I'd set one of the Teddies to studying and working soil full time. There is so much to learn and so many experiments a person could perform, it could take an interesting lifetime of concentrated effort and discovery to perfect the art of growing things.

The Lower Garden

The soil in the smaller lower garden I built from scratch. I started with the same dry lakebed concept, but instead of topsoil I filled it with many, many truckloads of wood chips, then added bulk amendments from there: clay and sand and composted weeds, leaves and garden scraps. I also used horse and cow manure. Later I limed it and added certain micronutrients like crushed eggshells, greensand, rock dust and cottonseed meal. I've also drenched it with fish emulsion, fertilizer solution and worm casting solution. Occasionally I'll go down to the lake and fish crappies for fertilizer too. One hot summer we had a huge trout kill. I buried a hundred or so trout in the garden down at Dad's and a few up here as well.

Kathy rotates her crops in our lower garden. Three years ago, she grew squash, two years ago it was potatoes, last year a year's supply of beans – and this year, lettuce, beets, Swiss chard, snow peas, onions and garlic. The beets and chard were stunted at first, but Teddy clone #2 started sifting through the umpteen million gardening books in the library and gleaning nutrient information and signs of specific deficiencies, and now they've perked up.

There are so many approaches to soil, from the petrochemical Republican to the organic Democrat. Then you have interesting spiritual rarities like Rudolph Steiner's biodynamics and also the Findhorn philosophy. Some cultures fertilize the soil with humanure, others preach against it. One guy likes to mulch the soil with newspaper, another doesn't. I think to a point it's all in what you believe, but I see nothing good in petrochemicals regardless of belief. It's my opinion that their fertilizers and pesticides are straight from hell. You might ask what Roundup-ready genetic manipulation, fed oodles of synthesized petrochemical fertilizers, could have to do with healthy, enlivened soil. My take is that it's profit-seeking, one-sided, insensitive, sit on your ass lazy selfishness.

I really need those clones. Teddies #3 and #4 would share a full time job: They'd spend their days on the deer trails scooping up deer shit, and near the mountain streams scooping up the rich pre-mixed forest loam where it collects in tiny pockets. They'd be the backpacker Teddies who then work that stuff into the garden soil – along with Teddies #5 and #6 who'd be hiking into the lowlands and the wilderness areas to pick paw paws, huckleberries, mushrooms, nuts, herbs and cranberries and drying them in the sun on the cliff outcroppings. Man, I'd like to have their full time job!

The Gold at Your Feet

There's no shortage of books with technical soil info. I don't see any point in plagiarizing them here. All I want to do is to get you to look at soil as you would a stock portfolio. Everybody's investing in gold these days but it's hard to chew, doesn't cook up real well and as far as I know you can't digest it. If some guy came up and gave me a couple of ounces of gold bullion and then got in his car and left, I'd call up the local construction firm to buy more topsoil before he reached the end of my driveway. People are buying gold like it's gonna save their asses. I've no use for gold. As far as I'm concerned only topsoil will save your ass.

Our (almost) Vegan Diet

Like everything else up here, the first garden was small and it just kept expanding in size. Now we figure we could survive on a basic Mexican peasant's diet. We've grown varieties of Indian flint corn that we grind up to make delicious sweet cornbread and pancakes. We've grown hard red winter wheat and quinoa. We've grown, dried, stored and eaten more kinds of beans than many people know exist: black beans, pinto beans, soybeans, both black and yellow (black soybeans make lavender-colored tofu), soldier, yin yang, brown beans, adzuki, cranberry, appaloosa and probably one or two others I've forgotten about. I'd like to try the Somerset bean. Nobody knows its origin, but the legend has it that a guy shot a wild goose and there were six beans in its craw. He planted them, they grew – and his name wasn't Jack.

Kathy and I are vegetarians. I came to it at age 17 when I shot my fifth deer. It was a good way off and it dropped to the ground. When I walked up to it, it lay not as if it was dying, but more as if it was taking a relaxing nap. It faced away from my approach. When I got within a few feet, it turned and looked me square in my eye with its entire snout blown clean off. That was it. I quit hunting and I couldn't swallow meat, any meat, including fish. Kathy quit eating meat a year after meeting me, though she's not as strict as I am. I'll eat a small portion of cheese to avoid offending a host, maybe an omelet in rare cases, but I always revert to my primary vegan diet, except for eating honey.

When Kathy makes tofu from scratch we look forward to the soysage (soy sausage) more than the tofu itself. Tofu is curded soymilk and okara is the pulp that's left after the milk is squeezed out of it. She adds sausage spices and stuff to the okara and steams it in a rice steamer. I've had young kids eat it, love it and never know it's not meat.

I remember one particular hearty breakfast she made on a Saturday morning – our own potatoes, our own soysage, our own corn flour pancakes topped with our own syrup (her pancake recipe is in Chapter 14). We've even made catsup, both green and red. That one single meal was infinitely more gratifying to me than driving a Porsche through town.

She grows several members of the crucifer family, three types of kale, kohlrabi, red and white cabbage. We also grow the typical things like carrots, peppers, tomatoes, horseradish, spinach, peas and green beans. And garlic (regular and elephant), onions, leeks, potatoes (red and white) and several kinds of winter and summer squash. This year I tended a purslane patch. Kathy's getting ready to make sauerkraut in the next few days. I did it last year. The two of us have for the most part a strict division of labor. I prep the soil. She's in charge of planting. I do the fruit trees, vines and berries and she does the vegetables.

Married Life

We're very much in love but can't stand to work *with* one another on anything. It's my fault, the result of my bad temper having pounced on her in her rare ditsy moments. Actually, I like her best of all when she does something stupid (her word) and claims she's a cross between Lucille Ball and Edith Bunker. I don't know what it is about those moments, but it really turns me on. When she's reflecting on her "shortcomings" and occasional ditsiness she's the absolute sweetest. That's when I'm most moved to kiss and hug her – maybe it's because her humility reveals a vast and breathtaking panorama between what she's thinking she is in that moment and what she really is. You see, she's really a level-headed true genius who came from a family of mere geniuses.

Ask her sometime about us having to pull one vehicle with another with a chain and catch it in gear to start the engine. She always drives the vehicle that pulls and I'm behind driving the one that won't start. We've done it so many times that it's resulted in every fiasco you could imagine. Some were downright dangerous. So my tractor's finally started and running and she's now pulling it faster than it wants to go with the truck and it skids sideways and I'm bouncing off trees. I'm back there screaming my head off, f-words flying everywhere, frantically waving my hands for her to stop. She keeps driving, and I can see in her rear view mirror that she's just watching a chickadee or something. As I'm about to pop an anger fuse with a rolled-over tractor on my lap, I just start laughing, so hard my belly hurts. I'll admit I can be just as ditsy and that I piss her off the same way in reverse, but I'm not gonna tell you about all those times.

Drying

We used to can a lot of fruits and vegetables but we've turned more and more to drying instead. In general, drying preserves much of what canning destroys in terms of nutrients. Occasionally it works in reverse but that's rare. Kathy cans tomatoes and salsa. She also cold packs (cans) the sauerkraut and the maple syrup. This year she canned applesauce. Every once in a while I'll step into the kitchen and make jam or pear butter, but for the most part my job is to do the drying. One year I was set up to dry about 54 pears every drying cycle – that's about every 24–48 hours. Sometimes Kathy dries her own celery and peppers. My methods of drying are elaborate, but she just slices them up, spreads them on a baking pan, sets them on the roof and hopes the birds don't drop aerial scat bombs on them.

The method I use most often requires the wood stove to be fired. In antique shops you can find a type of stovetop oven that doesn't have a heat source of its own. They have to sit on top of a heat source. I have four of them. They're basically metal boxes with windowed doors on the front and some racks inside

to bake on (see the how-to in Chapter 13). A wee bit of alteration makes them into perfect food dryers. If you keep the doors
cracked open an inch or so the hot air form the wood stove flows
up through the racks. I've also used a few different homemade
solar dryers. If the wood stove is going, Kathy will set her drying
pans somewhere near it, also depending on how hot it's burning.

Our Multi-functional Grinding Stones

We have three old sharpening stones we use on top of the wood
stove. They look like big wheels lying flat on top of each other
in tiers. They average about two feet in diameter and 2½ inches
thick. These are the wheels you see people grinding their axes
on in old Western movies. Part of the stone sits directly on the
wood stove. The surface of that single round stone does many
things. If you set a pot in one area it's a slow cooker, like one of
those crock-pots. If you want to culture yogurt overnight you
move it a good bit to the left. Another place is good for growing
yeast and there's a certain place that keeps your coffee or teacup
at the perfect drinking temperature.

Our Stoves: Beauty and The Beast

Sitting about four feet to the left of the wood stove heater (the
one we call The Beast) is a wood-burning cook stove. It was an
old hybrid stove that could use either gas or wood. I ripped out
all the gas guts because we have another complete gas stove in
the sugar shack. Later I learned these hybrids were really dangerous and you don't have to be a rocket scientist to figure out why.

This beautiful old stove is really heavy. I paid 35 bucks for it. A counselor from one of the five adjudicated youth facilities who brought kids up to visit came by with a few strong boys up to help me move it in. There was an adapter on the back of the stove that I had to remove to get it through the door. It's a cast iron elbow that makes a 90-degree turn out the back and straight up toward the roof. This cast iron piece is a 6-inch oval shape. The oval interfaces with the 6-inch circular stovepipe with an oval-to-circle adapter, which is the same gauge thin steel as the chimney flue pipe (like a real heavy-duty coffee can).

At any rate, I lost the damn thing for seven years. I looked everywhere for it so many times I started to question if it really did exist because you really could hook the stove up without it. If you did, the adapter would stick straight out the back, and the 90-degree turn would be made with the 6-inch circular stove-pipe. That would mean the stove would have to sit another foot or more out from the wall into the room. What I totally forgot was that I had taken it down to repair it in Dad's shop. I eventually found it in the barn down at Dad's under a table where Kathy and I had a landline phone and answering machine. Those years you had to walk a half-mile down the mountain to make a phone call.

Now we just love firing up this beautiful old cook stove in the early fall and late spring, before we fire up The Beast (the wood stove heater) and after we shut it down for the season. It takes the mild morning chill out of the house before the day warms up. We just kinda huddle around it in the cold morning before the sun rises and the day warms up.

The Beast itself is made from a turn of the century lard-rendering vat that I found in a junkyard down in Mt. Pleasant. My buddy Cal and I used to go down there and look for cool things to make stuff out of and then we'd send a pretty girl to ask the old guy what he wanted for it. That's how we got stuff cheap.

This vat was steam heated so it melted the lard out evenly and didn't char the fat. It was like a huge double boiler sealed with big hammered rivets around the top and bottom and up one side. I liked it because it looked so medieval. The hard thing was I had to cut the inner liner out to make it into a wood heater, so as to maximize the heat transfer from fire through the steel and into the room. If the heat had to travel through both steel walls (inner and outer) with an air space, it would have defeated itself as a heat source.

The rivets sealed the inner liner to the outer lining and I had to torch every rivet to get the damn thing apart. It took most of an afternoon. Every time I thought I had it cut loose I'd chain it to the end of the backhoe bucket and swing it around like a demolition ball. Then I'd try to whip it like a whip so the two pieces would come apart. Not an OSHA-approved technique.

Not only does The Beast heat the house, it heats the water and it enables the top grinding stone to do its magic. Kathy also does most of the cooking on it over the winter and someday soon I hope to slap one side of some Peltier crystals on it and draw the cold intake air from outside across the other side and produce some thermoelectricity. The greater the temperature differentiation between the two sides, the more electric power they will produce.

The door on the front of the stove was practically shoved in

Drying winter pears atop "The Beast" – grinding stone at left

Part of our maple syrup harvest cooling after the canning process

Canned tomatoes cooling atop the unlit wood heating stove

Wine bar and dish cupboard, made with reclaimed wood

my face by the guy who owned the builder's supply where I had gone to buy cement. He'd special ordered the door for someone who'd backed out on the sale. It wasn't the size I had in mind but I thought it would be cool to have a door with a tempered glass window. Because the glass isn't smooth – all you see is a warm glow of distorted yellows, oranges and reds, a bit like a window to hell. Every once in a while I clean the glass and enjoy the view from the security of my rocking chair. I have around 48 hours to ponder the weeping and gnashing of teeth before it goes totally black with soot again.

We call it The Beast because I wanted to build a wood stove that would really really produce heat if we needed it. Other stoves were borderline when it got really cold. The door itself has two nice air vents to control the heat, but I also have two 2-inch air vents on the lower back of the stove that have valves on them. They are piped through the floor and take air directly from the outside of the house (this is the air I'd use for thermoelectricity), whereas the air vents in the door are fed air from every unsealed crack in the doors and windows. I put these valved vents on The Beast in case of extreme frigid weather, when I've seen parts of the interior stone walls closest to the outside wall actually draw frost in on themselves.

Then came the test. It approached 35 below one night. I closed the front door valves, opened the frigid vents to stop all drafts and went to bed. Then Kathy walked over a bit later, saw the door vents were shut and opened them. Around 2 am we both woke up in a sweat, the whole house was like a sauna and it was 35 below outside. It passed the test.

The stove's other claim to fame happened during a four-day trip to New York City in late fall. Before we left, I cleaned out most of the ashes and then burnt a new fire to a good bed of coals. Then I packed it meticulously with huge halved and quartered bone oak logs. These are cut from big, dead standing oaks that long since shed their bark. They look like huge bleached dinosaur bones and are already quite seasoned and dry. Then I shut all the valves and opened one just a crack. We came back four days later to a small glowing bed of embers. Four days!

The Fireplace and Other Heat Sources

I've also acquired a few cheap common wood stoves that aren't airtight, taken them apart and made them airtight by sealing every crack and joint with a mixture of high temp fiber and cement. Initially they'd burn for six hours max. When I was finished they'd hold a fire for 24 hours. I've altered the air intake. It's all in controlling the air intake.

The fireplace is in our living room, which flows into the kitchen and dining room. It too is an integral part of our giant kitchen lifestyle. By that I mean that from a certain perspective this entire place and compound can be seen as one huge kitchen. There are times, seasons and circumstances that make us turn to the fireplace as the main heat source. Sometimes we do all the cooking and baking in it. We have one of those units that pivot in and out of the flames and adjust up and down as well. You often see the pioneer's wife using them in movies about the Old West. You can either hang a stew pot on it or send the frying pan or wok in over the flames. We also set the Dutch ovens directly in the coals. In the early years we had to carry a 20-pound propane bottle a half-mile up the mountain – deep snow in the dead of winter. Not our idea of having fun. One time we ran out of cooking propane and just got into cooking everything in the fireplace for weeks.

One of our food drying systems incorporates the fireplace heatilators that I made from four identically bent sections of two-inch exhaust pipes. The pipes double as a grate on the bottom, then they rise up the back and come out the top and to the front again. As the fire gets hot, the pipes suck cold air in the bottom and blow it aggressively out the top by the natural force/flow of convection. I have a metal table with four holes in it and four short pieces of flexible exhaust pipe. These four flex pipes shove into the top of the four heatilator pipes where the heat blast comes out, and go through the holes on the table and into the bottoms of the same box-like oven dryers I use to dry food on the wood stove.

When we want to take the morning chill out of the air or heat the house just a bit, we have our choice of four heating sources – the fireplace, the beautiful wood cook stove, the sunroom wood heater or the front room wood heater where we dry our clothes in winter. The Beast is for the dead of winter. We have another complete wood cook stove up in Wayne's World (the summer kitchen next to the wood shed, named after Wayne the cat). If Kathy's just baking cookies or pizza shells she might use the propane oven we have in the sugar shack. All three of the cook stoves (two wood and one propane) are off-white and that particular antique avocado green color that Kathy and I both love.

The Sugar Shack

We tap the red maple. Whereas the sugar maple takes around 35 gallons of sap to make one gallon of syrup, the red maple takes around 75 gallons to make a gallon. It's twice the sap, twice the work and it's twice as good as sugar maple.

If you taste sugar maple syrup beside red maple syrup you'd say that the sugar maple syrup has a bite to it. People describe our syrup as butterscotch toffee and some claim they taste a hint of chocolate in it. I love watching people's faces when I give them a teaspoon. I say, "First put a tiny drop on the end of your tongue and let that explode in your mouth. Then you can suck down the rest."

The sugar shack where we boil the sap has walls and a roof, but it's open on both sides toward the front. One opening side feeds the sap and the other feeds the firewood. Doors would drive you crazy. It has shuttered windows on two sides and high shuttered vents front and back. They all get opened when you boil so the moisture has someplace to go. The high back window opens to the morning sun. I have movies of a rolling boil in the morning, with the steam billowing up through the first shafts of light. Just beautiful. Under that window hangs some of my mask collection, mostly sunshine faces.

I've yet to learn to granulate syrup into sugar or make it into candy. Nonetheless, we use it in place of other sweeteners for everything from baking and winemaking to our coffee and tea. My very favorite thing is a rarity: Every so often I'll bring up a quart of syrup from the basement, and there in the center will be this big, clear crystal of pure sugar. It has no maple flavor, just pure sweetness. I can sit on the couch and suck on one for hours. Watch and you'll see my eyes start to glaze – say something to me and I won't answer.

It's nice to brew coffee and tea with spring water, but you haven't lived until you've made your coffee with tree water. It's indescribable. I think there's no more pure of a thirst quencher than tree water. From the first run of sap till the end of season the spring water jugs just sit there dormant.

You can buy out a company and increase your net worth 20-fold, but that kind of shit pales besides getting up at 5 am, firing up the tractor and going out in the woods to gather sap. I have a dipper I use if the collecting buckets are brim full. From tree to tree I take a long drafts of ice-cold tree water and from tree to tree I'm pissing in the woods. I never really heard of other people guzzling the stuff until someone sent me an article about how popular it is in Korea. Maple tree water sells for seven bucks a gallon in Seoul. They fire up saunas, eat a big bunch of salty nuts and stuff and try to drink five gallons of tree water and sweat it out their pores. Their goal is to replace all of the water in their body with tree water. The stuff is the purest of pures and it's full of minerals and nutrients.

Tapping trees and making syrup

Through the years of tapping trees I've came upon a neat way of doing it. It downsizes on the conventional holes by an eighth of an inch and it keeps all rainwater and bugs out of the sap collector. I use plastic 5-gallon food grade buckets for the job. I also use clear plastic tubing that has a quarter-inch inner dimension hole. I cut pieces of it about 14 to 20 inches long and for each one I slowly bring one end downward toward a burning candle flame until it melts, making something akin to an O-ring (or a mushroom) on the end. Then I use a good quality dual-size pencil sharpener, the kind mechanical drawers use, and shave the tubing's melted roundness into a kind of spear shape. The drill bit and the outer dimension of the plastic tube are identical. The little spear shape locks and seals the tubing in the holes drilled into the trees. I also just sharpen the other un-melted side of the tube with the pencil sharpener to make it easier to start into the hole on the bucket. It makes a tight, hermetic fit.

I drill three ⅝-inch holes in each 5-gallon collecting bucket in a line just below the lid and three holes per tree a little higher than the top of bucket. Then I connect everything together to start collecting sap. If I have a tree that produces a lot I'll add a fourth hole to the bucket to send the overflow to an auxiliary bucket. I don't know how many clips are on the lid to seal it to the bucket, but only ever click two on the collection buckets at the 9 and 3 hand of the clock. Use the same two clips points and it gets easier to work on and off.

Somebody brought me up a syrup maker's supply book. In it was a boiler/evaporator for beginners. It was for the backyard tree tapper who just wanted a new hobby. It cost around $795. I built my two production boilers for $15, plus a welding rod. One is made from a stainless steel salad bar unit that my buddy Bruce was using to mix cement in. It's a large, long tray with 4-inch-high sides. Some salad bars fill them half full of ice and then set their bowls of salad and fixing in it. The other similar

It's maple syrup time: some collecting buckets

*Tapping a red maple (note the overflow tube leading
to an auxiliary bucket)*

Boiling off the sap

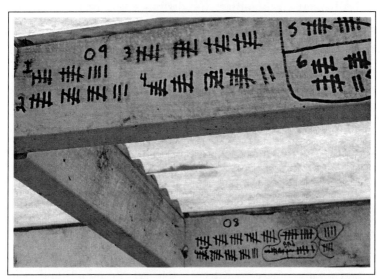

The rafters of the sugar shack: marking some very good years!

stainless unit was in a pile of junk where I bought the plastic manhole riser that sits on top of the methane tank. The workers at this supply yard were gonna make it into a shower stall base so the guys could shower at work before they went home. They sold it to me for $15.

These two stainless steel trays are about 2½ feet wide by 4-plus feet, and around 4 inches deep. They sit on top of two bases made out of an obsolete battery rack that Dad dragged home from work. There's a door on the front of both bases like a wood stove door where you feed wood into the fire. These units sometimes burn continuously for weeks at a time. I have to keep them too hot to touch all night, lest the bears come in and drink up all my hard earned sweetness.

All about on the rafters and doors are year marks – '92, '93, etc., and then from '00 on up. Beside the year are slash marks. Four I's crossed equals five 5-gallon buckets of sap that got poured into the boilers. I made enough three years ago to carry us through the last two years, and thank God for that, because we've had some unbelievable snowfalls. That would have made it really hard to get out into the woods. I hope next year to recruit some help and do a big season.

You've got to have strength and stamina to do this. For every 5-gallon bucket I handle I have to pick the 5-gallon collector up and pour the tree water into a 5-gallon transfer bucket. Then I carry the transfer buckets to the tractor and load them onto the trailer, then unload and stack the full buckets – and finally I have to lift each one up chest high and pour it slowly and carefully into the boiler so it doesn't splash out.

Pouring them in is the most strenuous of all.

I think '95 was the year I made 27 gallons of syrup. The sap was running for over nine weeks. We ran our 20-pound propane-cooking bottle dry at the end of that season and I asked Kathy to get it filled after work. She came home and I asked, "Did you get it filled?" She said, "It's in the back of the Justy (our Subaru)."

I had been lifting 47-pound buckets for nine weeks straight. I walked down to the Justy, reached in, grabbed the tank and gave it a sharp heave. The back of my hand zoomed up and hit the dome light so hard it smashed it to pieces and cut the hell out of my hand. After my nine-week workout it was like grabbing a cement block that no one told you was a fake one made out of Styrofoam.

Once we get the sap reduced close to the syrup stage we bring it inside and finish it in big stainless pots on the wood stove. We have this little one-ounce thing we call "the sippy cup." Its purpose is to taste test the syrup to see if it's ready to put into quarts and hot-pack it for storage, like you do when you can fruit and vegetables. What it turns into is a gain-five-pounds addiction. I don't know what heroin is like, but warm bordering on hot syrup in the sippy cup has got to come close. We used to use an expensive Polish refractometer to refine the syrup, but doing it by taste alone works beautifully – and much more delightfully. You're looking for that perfect cream texture that you have to scrub off your tongue against the roof of your mouth. A maximum linger of sweetness on the tongue.

Wine and Mead

I grow concord grapes, currants, blueberries, strawberries, hardy kiwis, apples, pears, red and yellow plums and two kinds of peaches. I grew up watching Dad make wine and we often helped. The basics are in me like genetics. Two years ago I made 85 gallons of wine to use up a bumper crop of fruit. There were 5-gallon glass carboys throughout the house. The CO2 bubbling in the air locks sounded like a bunch of clocks ticking softly out of synch.

Actually, I made fruit mead that year because I used clover and black locust blossom honey to amp up the sugar content. Mead is honey wine. As far as I know, and do, for that matter, I'd say all mead is wine. Wines are made from fruits in general, but we've made it with sugar beets and flower petals too. Wines are usually let to complete the fermentation process before bottling, whereas sparkling things like beer and champagne are bottled early. The bubbles in beer, champagne and some mead I've tasted are ones they shut the door on when they corked the bottle. They stay in there and wait till you pop the cap and they fizz forth.

Creating bubblies is an art and a science. Some drinks are let to ferment and then are recharged with a sugar and immediately capped. If it goes right, fermentation goes on up to a point, then it equalizes dormant lest the bottles burst. Too much food for the yeast makes champagne. Way too much yeast and the bottle will burst.

Wine is the art of drawing aroma and flavor from something and infusing it in a tasty, self-preserving liquid that'll give you a good buzz. Beer captures the savor of a sweet malted grain. I think I read somewhere that wines and beers were once seen as a way of putting up sustenance, more or less categorized with canning.

All you need is a good book to start out with and the supplies and equipment they call for. I use old polar water jugs to ferment in. You can buy the proper size cork for those jugs with a hole in it that accepts a common air lock or you can invent a seal and something to act as an air lock. On my alcohol fuel fermenters I just run the CO2 into a glass of water so it bubbles out but no air can get to the wine. Those who ferment in crocks rely on the "must" to keep the air out. That's the thick layer of fruit mash that rises to the top of the crock. Old timers used to cover the crock by just laying a board on it, no real air seal at all.

Pure honey mead and retsina are my all-time favorite drinks. Retsina is an acquired taste. You have to head into the outskirts of ancient Greek cities or countryside villages and find a taverna that takes it cloudy and unsettled right off the keg. It's a white grape wine stored in a pine keg, and it tastes a bit like turpentine at first. You have to like the taste of turpentine.

Other years I amped up my wine with maple syrup. The reason I want a 22% or more sugar content is that I use a high potency yeast, the same yeast I use to make alcohol fuel. I was told that Sam Adams bred up the super yeast to make a 40 proof (20% alcohol) beer. Fermenting with a super yeast can also yield a slightly sweet 40 proof wine, basically a brandy but without the work. Plus brandy relies on distillation and those kind of stills are illegal for the home brewer. I'm guessing you can also legally freeze the water out with similar results, but I don't know much about that. If you didn't do it in winter it would require a lot of energy.

Brandy is labor intensive because you first have to separate your brewed liquid into three components and dispose of one. You save the first, alcohol and the second, the condensed syrup-like flavored essence, and you toss out the third, the water, so it no longer dilutes the wine. Then you mix the alcohol with the condensed syrup. You basically undilute the wine and up the proof reading by distilling out the water.

Some yeasts and cultures are in the air but only indigenous to certain regions. A certain bacteria just happened to evolve in a certain area and it cultured milk a certain delightful way. Those bacteria were captured and cultured for generations. Many of the great cheeses came from indigenous conditions and so was the kombucha mushroom. I heard there are some places where you can culture yogurt with the air you breathe. I believe it. Once, a kombucha mushroom got into the air here in the house and grew on some of our food. It even grew on our salsa.

The one basic thing to understand about brewing is the nature of yeast. Alcohol is basically yeast piss. There are many types of yeast and they each have a specific piss tolerance, which is its alcohol percentage rating, from weak beer yeasts up to Sam Adams' Sampson yeast. By piss tolerance I mean how much of a concentrate of its own piss (alcohol) will kill it off and end fermentation.

Beer yeasts are weaker. Some die off in a 6% piss solution. So the concept to grasp is this: If you want a nice, neutral dry wine of about 14% alcohol, you get a 14% yeast and feed it an exact 14% sugar solution. If you want it real dry, feed it a sugar content slightly under the yeast rating. If you want a sweet 14% wine, use the same 14% yeast with a 15% and up sugar solution. The higher the sugar-to-percentage rating ratio, the sweeter the wine. When you're preparing the solution, before adding the yeast, all sugar solutions will give a percentage reading on the Balling scale of your wine hydrometer. Water is zero specific gravity. Any sugar – fruit juice sugar, honey, maple syrup, white, brown or raw sugar – affects the liquid's specific gravity.

Between Dad and me we've made at least 30 different wines. Some were elegant like French lilac or rose petal, but we never made dandelion wine. I clearly remember how horrible his pineapple wine tasted. We started bottling it and decided to just dump it out. Then we found a single aged bottle of it many years later and realized we made a big mistake. It was first rate.

When I was in high school Dad made an excellent huckleberry champagne. He and Mom were gone for the day so my buddy Charley and I skipped school. I snuck into their bedroom closet and stole a bottle. We were in the kitchen and when I opened it up it did what warm champagne does, it exploded. The pressed fiber ceiling tiles that had been white were now soaked with purple dye. Bad day – bad day – bad day!

In order of excellence, the best wines I've made are Concord grape amped with pure red maple syrup, winter pear amped with locust blossom honey, and red plum amped with clover honey. The Concord wine has excited many shouts of glee, like, "Now this is what wine was intended to be!" It was my favorite of all. One 5-gallon carboy produced a slightly hallucinogenic property in the wine. Never did a liquid roll and wave so easily across the tongue, down the throat and into the stomach. Never did an alcoholic beverage so stimulate the impulse to guzzle.

Other people had similar reactions to the winter pear and red plum wines. The plum was a sip and a savor and you breathed out fresh plums. The winter pear had a taste of heavenly bliss. There's so much alcohol in the yellow plum you have to sip it like whiskey. It's the out breath that I enjoy, the fragrance of the plum's freshness and sweetness, its essences, I guess.

I like the Concord drunk as new wine. I don't like it when it ages. One year however, a Concord aged itself into what some remarked was the finest Merlot they'd ever tasted. It had no bite to it whatsoever – the smoothest of smooths. The taste of a white Concord grape ripened to perfection to me is the taste of heaven. I made a white Concord wine last year and as a new wine it expressed that heavenly savor and so it disappeared fast, to say the least. I was saving a gallon for our very appreciative wine tasting friends Diane and Sarah. I opened it for a taste not long ago and to my dismay it had aged. It aged with grace, but I far prefer the new wine.

We've not dipped much into the peach wines because set beside the others they're intense in many regards. I have a feeling they might do what the pineapple did, at least I'm hoping they do. I think a little of that attitude came from when I stole a gallon of Dad's peach when I was a junior in high school. My buddy Todd and I sat in my old Jeep bull shitting about stuff and every few minutes you'd hear one of us saying, "Lemme talk to the man," which meant pass me the bottle. I got so sick I won't even describe what happened to me. Not pretty.

I couldn't become an alcoholic if I tried too. I have a weak stomach when it comes to drinking; therefore I was moved toward having other vices. A few years before the peach wine grabbed me I got real sick on beer. I can't say I've really ever enjoyed a beer since then, close to enjoyment, but not total.

I never got into making beer much, probably because of my sweet 16 experience and for the fact you have to buy so much and I don't grow grains. Years back, my anarchist buddy Paul tried to stir my interest by coming and brewing from scratch, and my two friends, Little Joe and Dr. Pete, brew good beer too and offer a little inspiration. But nothing ever stirred me as much as the other day when Kathy and I went to a beer distributor and I had my first experience of beer making's colorful and growing diversity. Walking down isles of microbrews lit up my brain. I was indeed all smiles! Maybe there's a new project for my list.

I'd better put down my glass and move on. The next chapter deals with refrigeration and the off-grid alternatives for The Stone Camp.

10

REFRIGERATION

*"I got the idea from seeing some air vents on the mountain
along the north side edge of Jack Hollow..."*

✃

I'm approaching three different types of natural, green refrigeration – well actually four. Numbers 1 and 2 are working now, and 3 and 4 have to do with winter ice storage and methane gas.

Peltier crystals
The first working refrigeration has to do with Peltier crystals. Those are the working piece inside the 12-volt refrigerator units that plug into a cigarette lighter. I first saw them at truck stops where truckers were using them in their big rigs. Now they're common. We use them from time to time in the house and often when we go for a long drive in the car.

On some of these units you can switch the electric polarity and change the unit from a cooler into a warmer. I've picked up a bunch of them at the flea market. Most look like common picnic coolers, but I also have two that look like miniature upright refrigerators, and two that look like tiny polar water dispensers. I have one that holds and cools just a fifth wine bottle, and I have two that will clutch an aluminum pop or beer can and cool just that. It's definitely green refrigeration in our case, because they're powered by sun and wind.

The neat thing about the Peltier crystal gut in these units is that you can convert them to generate electricity with heat. There's a big heat sink that's supposed to get rid of heat, but if you feed it heat instead, it makes electricity. It becomes a thermoelectric generator. It's been said that this is the only source of electrical power generation that will not be affected by a freak intense solar flare. Everything else will get fried (except our brains, I hope).

I've gutted out four of these Peltier crystal units so far in order to morph them into a bigger unit that will produce power from either methane or my wood stove. Minus the huge aluminum heat sinks (heat dissipaters) the working unit is only about 2" x 2" x ¼". These 12-volt refrigerator units are becoming so common, I've even seen one dumped along the side of a road. If you ever come across one for a few bucks or so, pick it up for me, gut it out and send me the crystal with the red and black wires still attached. I could use a bunch of them and I'll reimburse you, for sure. On second thought, maybe you won't need to bother. I just found out that the crystals themselves can be bought cheap online.

Crude geo-cooling

I remember the coffee buzz that brought this one on and even the chair I was sitting on. I got the idea from seeing some air vents on the mountain along the north side edge of Jack Hollow, adjacent to our place. I noticed that in winter the vents melt all the snow around them and in the summer the air flowing out of them feels cool. Next thing you know Ted's on the backhoe ripping the hell out of things again, making an underground storage chamber that self-regulates its temperature year-round.

As I was building the chamber I made a discovery, using many sticks of incense. Up near the sugar shack, where the chamber is, are two PVC 90-degree couplers hooked together sticking up out of the ground. They look like an upside-down J-shape made of 4-inch plastic pipe. That's so rain doesn't go down the pipes where the air enters.

After I finished the system I held incense at this entrance at different times when the ambient air temperature changed. At 50 degrees nothing happened, no air/smoke went in the entrance. That's because there's no reason for it to sink, because ground temp (constant 50 degrees) and air temp at 50 degrees are in a state of equilibrium. As the air cools, it gets heavier and wants to sink all by itself. So at 60 degrees the incense showed that it started to suck in just a little air. By the time the air temperature reached 90 degrees it became a real aggressive sucker.

Imagine it! All by itself, by a simple force of nature, an increase in temperature differentiation makes the unit work harder when you need it most. I didn't foresee this, nor did I foresee that in the winter it reverses and the air flows uphill, because warm air rises. We have stored root crops in this system's cooling chamber and currently I age vinegars in it. Kathy suggested recently that we store grains and beans in it too. The entrance to it is through a door close to the ground.

Another story: It happened that our dogs had been erupting into fierce barking for two nights in a row. The second night I walked out with a flashlight and saw my first fisher. I didn't even know what the hell it was till I looked it up in a book. It's a really big member of the weasel family that was introduced because it's the only animal that knows how to kill a porcupine without getting pierced with its needles.

The third day we had been out shopping and had bought a big chunk of aged provolone cheese. It was still waxed and wrapped with cord so I took it out and hung it in this cooler. That night the dogs woke us, roaring again. I came down to see what was upsetting them and remembered that cheese *(Yum, I'm gonna go out and cut off a chunk)*.

I walked out the back door in my underwear, salivating. I had a paring knife in one hand and flashlight in the other, scanning the ground for snakes. I got to the cooler, bent down to open the door, and felt a sudden wind over my back and then one quick instant earthquake.

There was a bear, maybe 500-plus pounds, sitting on top of the cooler wondering where the hell this wonderful smell of cheese was coming from. The wind and the quake made me stand up so quick I almost toppled back right into him. By the time I jerked my flashlight up to see what the hell just happened, all I saw was his huge massive butt running away as fast as he could. Then I heard my electric fence wires snap as he plowed right through them. I don't know who was the most scared. The reason I know he was scared is because every bear that ever wandered in cried like a baby when I'd push them towards the electric fence.

The Icehouse

The icehouse is a work in progress. This icehouse is like the old-fashioned ones in some ways, but it's also an entirely new and unique concept. This one will be like a super-insulated beer cooler – 7 feet wide by 8 feet high by 19 inches long – but it will house my own personal chunk of glacier instead of a 6-pack. I'll fill it with ice in the winter, shut its doors and maybe never open it even once during the summer. All I'm interested in is the glacial melt, the constant 32-degree drip as the ice melts. That drip is what I'll use to refrigerate, not the ice itself. I also plan on being able to accelerate that drip to a tiny, steady stream by venting in ambient air, especially if I need to cool a case of beer real quick.

The actual user part of the system will be an insulated grotto similar to the geo-thermal airflow cooling system's. Only when you open the door on this one you'll see a big chunk of pink granite sticking up like a miniature mountain out of a miniature pool of glacial melt water. The pool itself will be shallow in some places and maybe somewhere as deep as a fifth of wine is tall.

Granite is igneous, with a very dense molecular structure. I'm thinking that granite will do what a heat sink does, but in reverse. I can't see how it wouldn't just absorb the coldness into itself and then emanate it outward. Did you ever pick up a heavy piece of steel in winter with your bare hands? It's holding so much coldness that it hurts. The floor is going to be the steel frame of a salvaged truck bed. Since I needed a place to clean, paint and store the truck bed, I first went ahead with laying a permanent concrete foundation and set the frame in place.

I found and bought about 45 linear feet of 6-inch-thick foam panels that originally lined a walk-in freezer. They will be for the interior walls. My icehouse will be double-walled with about an 18-inch gap between. The outer wall will be, at very least, a wood shell. Ideally, it will be plastered with one of the new exterior finishes applied over a shell of 2-inch Styrofoam. The gap between the walls will be filled with an ocean of uni-formly chipped-up flakes of Styrofoam cups, platters, packaging and miscellaneous scrap.

Submerged in this ocean will be a number of "mined sub-marines," the compacted blocks I described in Chapters 7 and 8, placed strategically here and there and set to explode and expand slowly so as to compact the Styrofoam chips. Styrofoam is made of the same #2 and #4 plastic as the plastic wrap. It's that plas-tic that has the microscopic air chambers in it. As my blocks expand they will have air chambers too, but not microscopic. That's why I figure the expanded plastic blocks will insulate near to as well as the Styrofoam.

I also hope to use a kind of space age super insulation between the double-layered floor of this icehouse. My cousin saw a demonstration given by a guy that sells it and said it's like magic. I was told that it comes both in paint or rolled sheet form. I've neither the name of the product nor do I know of a supplier. If anybody could help me out here I'd appreciate it.

Now a neat coincidence is that the underground airflow refrigeration intake (the upside-down J from my geo-thermal cooling chamber) is only a few feet from the lower left of the icehouse, where the melt-water grotto will be. That means I can further extract the coolness and send it down the air pipes. All I need to do there is to direct the overflow water from the grotto into an automobile radiator, extract it with a low wattage 12-volt muffin fan and send it into the air intake. This icehouse project, I'm telling you, is gonna be the coolest of cools!

Converting a propane refrigerator to methane

The fourth refrigeration system, one for the near future, is simply to convert a propane refrigerator to run on the methane gas that we produce here at The Stone Camp. I know it has been done. A propane refrigerator runs on a candle-sized flame of burning propane. That flame boils ammonia in an enclosed refrigeration loop. It refrigerates at the top where the ammonia vapors re-condense. After I first oxidize and clean some of the caustics like sulfide out of the methane, I'll convert the refrigerator to run off of a methane flame instead. I also have to set up my compressing system to store winter methane when the fridge is shut off.

And where do I plan to get the methane? The answer lies in what most people call their "sewage system." That's coming up next.

11

WATER

"When the springs are dry, our systems will be sustaining us."

In the future, we're going to be hearing more and more about water pollution, water scarcity and drought. I'm sure wars are gonna be fought over water. It's the natural result of the way civilization has used and abused this limited and absolutely essential resource. Kathy and I have been aware of this for a very long time. Over the years, I've figured out a number of highly efficient techniques for collecting, processing and purifying water. The result is a multi-purpose water system that allows water to fulfill its natural cycles. We don't waste water here at The Stone Camp, but we do have a continual supply that doesn't rely on wells or springs, although we do have access to two springs for drinking, cooking and the dogs' water. When longer and longer droughts occur, as we expect they will, we will be able to weather them. When the springs are dry, our systems will be sustaining us.

When we started living here, when all we had was the

springs. Crude rainwater collection was one of the first things we did. Even after years of elaborating on rainwater collection, we always felt we had the most insecure source of water. Over time we experienced a few intense droughts that lasted several weeks, periods when everyone's spring and well had run dry and people were trucking in water. Even when there was a little cloudburst, like an inch, it didn't replenish any of the ground sources for water. We, however, collected huge amounts from even these little cloudbursts. What we saw surprised us and made us see that we now had the most secure of systems.

Our utility water is rainwater that is lightly filtered and modestly disinfected. It settles out its minute particulates naturally in just hours after pumping. This water is used for the kitchen and bathroom sinks, the automatic washer and both hot tubs and showers – and man, is it nice to shower in. With the recent installation of the water pressurizing system needed for our alcohol distillery, we now have the potential to use reverse osmosis filters. Relying less on our springs as we use the filtered rainwater, we will be relying more and more heavily on our cisterns, but we right now have the capacity for it, and it's ever-increasing.

When I say we don't waste water, I mean that absolutely all water that we use in the house finds further use in our system, save the one-gallon flush from our Swedish IFO toilet. For the sake of definition, gray water is what comes from the sinks, showers and laundry machine. Black water is what comes from your toilet. Most people's gray and black water go to the same place, either the septic tank or the sewage treatment plant. In our system they are treated separately. The gray water goes through 10 in-ground filters that are for the most part invisible in the landscape. The black water feeds a methane digester modeled after ones that are designed and used in China. Over there, a mixture of pig and human poop will supply all the cooking and lighting gas for three households. Methane is one of nature's miracle energy sources.

The gray water and black water systems were legally installed according to what ordinances were in place in the '70s and early '80s. I can't legally do such things now because of stricter ordinances. Mine are only legal under a kind of grandfather clause. I'm all for the state passing more strict laws under the assumption that everybody is just gonna try to get away with something, that the only possible inclination anyone can have is to dump their shit into the stream. I mean that's just what most people do, unfortunately. But the thing is, as far as I know, there's no place in their mentality for someone who'd be inclined to meet and even exceed their requirements on their own without being forced to.

The state requires strict conformity to any one of the super-expensive treatment systems that they condone. I can't afford to import a couple of tons of specially crushed glass to fill a specially designed fiberglass tank and I don't know many people who can. I see all this money going to fund casinos, sports stadiums and other such endeavors and I'm thinking "Wow! that might be enough to make most streams drinkable again."

I'd stand my systems against anything the state requires. It can be done. A while back, we applied for a permit to put a causeway across the stream at the base of our driveway. My brother-in-law drew up the design and we submitted it for approval. It was so exemplary a design that the state asked to use its 19.5 yards of concrete blueprint as a model for others. I would hope that my affordable treatment systems would have the same fate but, considering some of the other experiences I've had with officialdom, I'm not holding my breath.

Starting Any Project: a Pep Talk

If you're contemplating constructing systems for your gray water and black water, but the whole idea seems overwhelming or even paralyzing, I'd like to offer a pep talk here about approaching problems. I believe that everybody's brain is the ultimate super computer if it's programmed correctly and not blocked by dysfunction and poor self-image. You can set it to any number of tasks and problems. All you do is clearly feed it the problem, sit back, be patient and don't even sweat an anxious mental drop. If you can do that, you'll find yourself sitting right up in your bed at 3 am and out of a deep sleep saying, "Oh, that's how it should work, that's how it should be done." I've found that when you're too busy obsessing about a problem, you can't hear inspiration ringing the doorbell to your brain.

My advice is to clarify the problem, as opposed to search for the solution. That's because the solution is really within the problem, not outside and separate from it. The gray water system program, to give a prime example, is perpetually working (not agonizing) in my brain. It has already gone through one major upgrade designed to deal with earlier flaws, and in another five or 10 years I hope to try a few new ideas and even increase its efficiency and zero maintenance aspect.

"Good enough for now" is a profanity to me. I don't like to wait for things to go wrong or fail. Instead I work to elaborate designs a step ahead of failure. I'm also inclined to design such overkill into projects that they dare not even think about failing. The methane system's effluent filter I'll describe shortly is an example of overkill.

Gray Water Treatment

We have a system that perpetually processes our utility water. Our gray water flows through three clarifiers, four aggregate filters, three living pools and finally trickles through the compost pile – and this year seeps into the Swiss chard at the head of the lower garden. The first installation of the gray water treatment plant presented a minor problem with grease and particles, and with grease clinging to particles. There was a trap I had to clean every five years or so. My first upgrade eliminated that. I'll describe the system as it is now and how I dealt with the earlier problem.

The three clarifiers are standing 75-gallon plastic olive drums. These were part of the first upgrade. All three do different things with the gray water to clarify it. When the water from our drains enters filter drum #1, it's directed in such a way that it swirls it in a vortex. There are baffles in all three so that only the cleanest water of each process exits from one and enters the next.

When the water reaches filter drum #3 it is released in the bottom and exits near the top. Filter drum #4 lies horizontally and is filled with huge chunks of lava rock. It also acts as a surge tank so the next three aggregate-filled vertical drums (#5, 6 and 7) can take their good old time doing their job. Number 5 is filled with crushed lava rock and #6 and #7 are filled with aggregate (stones) that get smaller and smaller until the water has to percolate through sand and then fine road ash.

I was just starting to assemble these filters to percolate the water downward through the aggregate when I was suddenly struck with the logic of percolating the water upward from the bottom, so I changed their design in mid-project. The upward flow accentuates the cleansing effort because of the tendency of impurities to settle down. That meant I had to pack the aggregates into their drums in reverse, with larger grade on the bottom and graduating to a finer grade on top. At the bottom of each aggregate filter is a black 4-inch donut-shaped pipe. It's a special, flexible, perforated leach field pipe designed to release water into a leach field. That's how I released the water at the bottom so it percolates up toward the top.

Filters #8, 9, and 10 are living pools. They each contain various plants that I introduced into them, plus others that seeded themselves. Currently, after the water flows consecutively through the roots of the plants in these three pools it enters the center of our main compost heap. These are made from those common little plastic wading pools that you see for sale outside Wal-Mart and Kmart. Each pool is double lined, so really I used six of them. The water is released into one and collected at the other end to be transferred to the next through an inch-and-a-half PVC pipe. At first the transfers didn't work until I discovered there was an airlock in each pipe. A small hole remedied that, but that hole had to be protected from anything that might clog it. A plastic dish scrubber clamped loosely over the hole did the trick.

Apparently, the gray water was quite appetizing to one bear who ripped off the lid of one of the drums to drink it up. I guess it's filled with nutrients too, because some of the growth in particular plant species in the pools borders on scary. I once saw the biggest coltsfoot leaf I ever saw in my life growing out of one of the pools. Normal ones are maybe 6-8 inches wide. This one was about 18 inches wide.

If you're only doing dishes or taking a shower, no water actually comes out the very end of the system in summer. It's all taken up by the plants and transpired into the air.

Preparing for drought

The whole gray water system is designed for a quick change in the event of a severe drought (which I do foresee is coming). When that happens, the living pools are no more. Instead, I will tap onto the last pipe that comes out of the last aggregate filter and direct that flow to an inch-and-a-half PVC Y-joint with two valves. One valve will open to a set of filters I have that will prepare the water for reuse as utility water (wash, sink, shower). The other valve will send it through a much more aggressive filtration system that will make it potable and drinkable.

In my manic eccentricity I've been collecting filters for

Gray water clarifier drums –
Filters #1, 2 and 3

Filters #8, 9 and 10 –
the living pools

Filter #4: horizontal surge tank

Three aggregate filters: #5, 6 and 7

An example of distribution/transfer, to be covered with a gravel-filled plastic feed sack

30-odd years. I have every kind imaginable: diatomaceous earth, sand, charcoal, every type of sediment filter and ones that remove all chemicals. I have five of every kind that filter drinking water. I have three reverse osmosis systems and even one that was modeled after the space shuttle's system that will filter urine so you can drink it (don't think I'll try that). One brand new reverse osmosis system I have retails for $700. Another, a new Kenmore, costs between $400 and $500. The third is a compact unit. I don't know what that one costs new. Now get this: I paid a total of around $15 for all three at the flea market.

There is a culture of people who buy out estates. The stuff they get from cleaning out the houses and garages is their inventory to set up and sell. They amass so much inventory that they have to turn it over quick and cheap. In the case of these reverse osmosis filters, they had no idea what they had and sold them for dirt.

Utility water system for the kitchen and for drinking

As I said, our utility water source is rainwater and it's great for showers and such, but not for drinking. At most, we'll brush our teeth with the hot water faucet in the bathroom because we know it's close to boiled. Our drinking and cooking water is, for the moment, still from the springs. We'll soon be able to produce potable drinkable water from rainwater too.

Our first elaborated water system was a platform about four and a half feet off the ground. On it sat four brand new plastic garbage cans plumbed together in such a way that as you filled one you filled them all. Then we simply ran a garden hose from it to the kitchen sink. In winter we'd bring in two of them and set them about 18 inches above the floor level. Then we'd bring the rainwater from the gutter through the window to fill them up.

Underground cisterns

But things developed, and now I have cisterns everywhere, five underground so far, four above ground, soon to be buried, and four to remain above ground, including the mobile water buffalo. The main one that sits underground above the upper cabin holds 1,500 gallons. It gives the house about 14 psi water pressure. We formed and poured it with concrete from 7am one day to midnight, non-stop mixing.

Sitting beside the main cistern is a 750 gallon one that I just installed. It's plastic with a poured concrete cap. The others hold 250, 1,000, 750, 400, 450, 500 and 300 gallons each. And I just got a big one that must at least be 3,000 gallons. That one's slated to become our swimming pool. I look around at this underground cistern system and think of Masada, the Jewish fortress in the desert that also had many cisterns.

Leaves and particles are mildly filtered through screens and then we rely on the settling-out process. By then it's pretty clean and clear. Old-timers used to throw alum in their cisterns to settle it quickly but that scares me. Occasionally I toss in a minimum amount of pool chlorine to kill any harmful stuff. I don't drink the utility water because birds shit on the roof. People have drunk it by mistake and they didn't die. Recently, I picked up a few ultraviolet units at the flea market. They will kill most harmful organisms. It would be nice to just switch one on in a cistern for a minute every once in a while and eliminate the use of chlorine.

The reason I said we're about to be able to drink cistern water is that I just installed a pressurizing system to feed the distillery coils. I needed the same system to drive water through reverse osmosis. Basically, we're tired of carrying spring water for the dogs. And if we do get the big drought we're ready.

Black Water

Black water is what comes from our toilets and cannot be introduced into the gray water system. I want to talk about toilets first. If and when severe drought hits, no more one-gallon flush Swedish IFO toilet. I'll switch to using only our commercial-bought compost toilet. But I'm working on another idea:

A fiberglass compost toilet

Out back I have a bunch of prefab cut pieces of fiberglass. They get rosined together to make the ultimate high capacity compost toilet. I really would like to get this one certified through some legal process if possible.

The pieces are cut out of two floor-to-ceiling shower stalls, one floor-to-ceiling bathtub stall, and one bathtub – all fiberglass. They're ready to go together like a transformer robot. This one is modeled after a Swedish Clivus Multrim compost toilet, with no moving parts. Instead, it's a slow-moving glacier of poop and vegetable matter moving on a certain-degree slope of smooth fiberglass. It slides down the fiberglass and hits a baffle that begins to break it down a bit. Then it falls into a finishing chamber, where it completes the composting process. That's the basics, but I've added my own touches to the design.

One big problem to solve was a heat source. That one smooth slope had to be slightly heated from time to time. I brainstormed many ideas, some very elaborate and involved. I thought of using hot air, which would involve fans and ductwork. I also considered using hot liquid pumped from the wood stove.

I programmed my brain to watch for the answer to this one, pushed enter and let it run for a few years. Then finally one day, as I closed the hatchback on our old Subaru Justy my eyes fixed on the heated back window. Transferring just electricity by itself is a hell of a lot easier than moving air or water (which also require electricity). So often a lot of potential power just goes to waste up here because I can't even come close to using it all. If I could pump it back into the grid I'd always be ahead and they'd be paying me.

My other option is a load dump: The computerized charge control box is what handles the power coming in from the sun and wind (see the next chapter on the power systems). You can adjust it to send the excess power to a workload such as a water-heating element, small space heater, or to running vent fans. I've got all the pieces of the huge compost toilet cut into its pre-fab pieces. I fit/clamped them together to make sure everything fit together. It's all thought out and can be quickly assembled. When I'm ready, I'll go to the junkyard and get the biggest electric grid heated back window I can find. Once I've rosined the toilet parts together I'll program a load dump to direct some excess power to that heated back car window, which I will have fiberglassed into the smooth slope down which will flow the glacier of poop and a few veggie scraps.

The methane digester

My septic/methane digester tank is a large, 375-gallon spherical plastic tank. The system is plumbed anaerobic. That means no air. My cousin Boo machined 4-inch plastic compression fittings for it on his metal lathe. No doubt his carbide cutters were feeling like superman. The fittings bolted on with stainless hardware and have huge thick O-rings to ensure a good seal. When the toilet is flushed into it, the 4-inch pipe is sent into it and turns at an angle so the flush constantly pushes the slurry counterclockwise.

There's a small pipe that sticks vertically out of the ground next to it to access an effluent water trap in the plumbing. It's like the one you see in the drain under your sink but bigger. It's a 3-inch pipe with a threaded cap. From there I can test the pH of the effluent. When I finally go into all-out production of methane I'll first send the wash water from one or two laundry cycles into the digester to boost the alkalinity. The methane bacteria like a neutral solution, as opposed to an alkaline solution, but alkaline must be added to bring the acidic slurry up to neutral.

Looking at the tank, there's a circular aluminum ring, which is the top of the "overkill" filter I spoke about earlier. This handles the gallon of water that comes out of the tank when a gallon is flushed in. The state requires a leech field for this if the ground passes their percolation test. If the test fails they require an expensive sand mound. From there it gets worse.

In appearance, the filter resembles an enormous urn. It's like a giant clay pot, but instead of being made of ceramic, its 18-inch-thick walls and 2-foot-thick bottom are made of rock dust. This stuff hardens like cement as it goes through many wet-dry cycles like rain or the hose, but it still remains pervious to water, much like a ceramic water filter. The urn is then filled with about four and a half feet of sand and then four feet of what's called shot gravel, crushed to the texture of the BBs in Kathy's Red Ryder Special (her hero was Annie Oakley). Before I backfilled around it to keep dirt and clay from clogging and corrupting it, I wrapped the entire thing in old synthetic carpet.

So that's my methane digester's effluent filter. I can access it directly beyond the digester itself. I basically pour anything down that filter except petrochemical solvents like gasoline oil or paint thinner, and of course my excess refined plutonium and petrochemical solvents like gasoline oil or paint thinner. I wash water-based latex paintbrushes and rinse out the organic garden sprayers into it, kaolin clay base, soaps, copper sulfate, all bio-fungicides and sulfur bases. I have great faith in this aggressive filter. The digester itself is equally and oppositely sensitive to contaminants.

Seeds of a great idea

Working down at Dad's is where I learned about methane. He needed his old steel septic tank pumped out, so we dug open the lid to expose its 3-inch threaded steel cap. The truck arrived and

I watched as the driver pulled out his vacuum hose, only to find he needed a 4-inch hole.

I said, "I'll have to torch it open for you." And then I asked the guy (the professional), "Do you think it's safe? He said, "Oh hell yeah, in 25 years I've never seen anything explode." First we unscrewed the cap and cut enough far enough outside the 3-inch hole so he had and extra half-inch to work with all around. I fired up the torch, set it on the mark and watched for the metal to start glowing red. Then I squeezed the oxygen trigger.

The very instant I first burnt through the steel all this methane ignited and blue flame came out the 3-inch hole with the deafening roar of a small jet engine. It just scared the living shit out of everybody. We ¾ dove and were ¼ pushed back by the compression. I hit the ground and covered my head. I saw some people run for their lives and others come running out of the house to see what just happened.

That's really the primary reason I have a methane digester, as opposed to a conventional system. That was the seed, and after that, I'm telling you straight-faced, the methane digester built itself. Just like so many things do around here.

From the moment my original system began to fail I experienced a growing dread of having no real nice thing to say about my sewage system. When people came to see the place I anxiously hoped they wouldn't ask me about it. Now I love to talk about it. The most unbelievable thing in its building itself was an email from my buddy Matt. He told me to "Look on these websites and tell me if you're interested. I found one of these in a ditch"(not literally). I pulled them up and here was a flammable gas compressor that could compress up to 300 psi. It turns out that any individual is allowed to compress a flammable gas up to around 300 or 350 psi. Many flammable gases are compressed into the 1,000's, but you have to be schooled and licensed for that.

I wrote back and said, "I'm interested, what did the guy use it for?" He wrote back and said, "Methane." Here I was in mid-project and this compressing unit, which I'm sure I never had enough in my checking account for, just came to me. It's how the entire system made itself. I remember no laboring or mental anxiety. Nor do I remember being overwhelmed at any point. It was driven by necessity. It may be that I was in, or aligned with, the great mind whose design in creation is based on necessity, instead of just my neurotic Ted brain. Not my will, but thy greater will that can manifest a gas compressor out of thin air through a friend. My life is like a spontaneous domino effect of needs being met.

12

POWER

"Our very first electric system consisted of pulling the car up to the window, popping the hood, clipping two wires on the battery terminal and watching our 5-inch black and white TV-radio."

⌀ℓℓ

Candles, propane, oil lamps, matches and disposable batteries are what we started out with. It's a wonder we're not dead from fumes. We also tried olive oil lamps, but with little success. Everybody thinks candles are so wonderful and natural, but in some dictionaries paraffin and kerosene have the same definition. It's just like the difference between the solid Crisco vegetable oil and the liquid vegetable oils. If you've got piles of money you could buy beeswax or bayberry wax candles to light your home, but a 35-year supply would break anybody's bank account. You'd have to work just to buy candles. Clearly, we had to get some kind of electric system going for us.

Our electric system is what's called a hybrid system because it integrates two sources of power: #1, wind and #2, solar. We're just now taking a leap into a four-source system, and as time passes it can easily evolve into six. In my speculative imagination I see the possibility of eleven.

Source #3 is ethanol 190 proof, for internal combustion engines. The first engine I plan to convert is the 12 h.p. engine on my battery charging generator (full descriptions of the still and battery conversion are given below).

Source #4 is thermoelectricity. Ethanol, methane and wood are all members/candidates of the thermoelectric family for us, but you can generate electricity from any heat source. This uses the Peltier crystals described the Refrigeration chapter.

Source #5, methane, is now available here and is being developed. You can cook with it and also fire thermoelectricity. I have a 2KW generator that will run on it.

Source #6 is wood gasification, my favorite – capable of powering anything from huge, many-thousand h.p. engines, down to 5 h.p. engines. We've already had five test runs on our gasifier. In this chapter I'll have a lot to say about wood gasification.

Source #7 is human power (a bike with a 12-volt alternator). Mother Earth News offered plans for one of these. It's basically comprised of a stripped-down 10-speed bike, a 35 amp car alternator and an old Type 1 VW (Beetle) flywheel. I believe the average person biking it in 5th gear can produce 5 amps 12-volt at a comfortable pace and 20 amps at a heart-pumping sprint. My Indian friend Michael has built generator bikes using rare earth magnetic charging technology.

Source #8 is a hydrogen cell. Depending on finances, I'd like to develop this form of power one day. It's a battery that when charged (in my case by wind and sun) breaks down water into hydrogen and oxygen. Methane is said to be the cleanest burning of the organically formed gasses, but hydrogen is probably cleaner if you don't consider what's involved developing it (building solar panels, windmills and the hydrogen cell itself). Hydrogen's nowhere near as caustic as methane, so I can compress and store it without worrying about the compressor and storage tanks oxidizing (rusting out).

Source #9 is steam generation. Years back, a place called The Steam Outlet offered plans for a 5 h.p. steam generator you could actually install on your wood stove. I've tried to locate those plans for years but so far haven't. I do know that the actual generator is made from a particular automobile pollution control pump and so many feet of half-inch bendable copper pipe coil inside your stove pipe. It also drives a car alternator.

Source #10, hydropower, wouldn't work up here because we have no mountain stream, but would down at my dad's, since his place sits beside one. I picked up two boat propellers specifically for the purpose in case I do get to it, and a while back rummaging through a barn sale I found an ancient "water motor" with common hose fittings on it. I tried it on my dad's pressurized outside garden hose and it spun with frightening speed.

Source #11 is biodiesel. I can see #11 taking place within a few years. My buddy Mike gave me his old biodiesel plant, so all we'd need to do is buy a new, high quality, single cylinder diesel

AC generator, build it a house and be done with it. If it really got hot out and I really wanted to air condition a tiny room 24/7 that's what I'd use for sure.

Wind Power

Our very first electric system consisted of pulling the car up to the window, popping the hood, clipping two wires on the battery terminal and watching our 5-inch black and white TV-radio. That's all we had for years. Then a friend who stayed here for a year or so bought me a $500 wind generator as a gift when he left. I put another $250 into this system, mainly for a one-yard concrete pour for the windmill's base and a bit more for its three dead men (solid underground concrete coffins) that anchor the guy wires.

I had already spent several years collecting (scrounging) all the guy wires and their cable clamps in anticipation of building my own windmill. My control panel was reworked from a big chunk of obsolete industrial trash. The first batteries I used were free, used NiCad wet cells. They were never really cycled that much, so they still had a lot of life in them (but once I learned of their toxicity I wanted them the hell out of here).

I built the first 40 feet of the tower from scratch. The additional 35 feet was an earlier failed tower someone had that had toppled in a tornado. I spent a lot of time straightening it back out and never got it perfectly straight.

A story: Skiing, quick drawing with a pistol and tracking are three cool things I always knew I was really good at…maybe fishing too. I'm also the kind of guy who brings his hard hat to work but never puts it on his head.

One afternoon I went down to weld on the first 40-foot section and I had my steel-toed leather boots with me, but not on my feet. I remember clearly the teaspoon-and-a-half of molten steel that was building up in the pocket of a certain weld. I also remember the sort of dam breaking that released that molten steel, like a tiny waterfall. It instantly burned through my tennis shoe, running between my big toe and the one next to it.

I danced and screamed. It burnt nearly to the bones. But what pissed me off more than anything was the national news story that night of a somewhat credible Bigfoot sighting nearby (very rare in this area). The guy who told about it was night fishing when he smelled a very strong odor before "it" actually walked up close to him. He even confessed that he pissed himself. And here I was with the skill and know-how to prove or disprove his claim, at least to myself, but I was unable to walk, let alone do a short hike into the gorge where the sighting occurred and study tracks.

Erecting the tower

The tower at the base is on a huge, heavy-duty hinge that pivots on a 2-inch-thick steel pin that's about two feet long. It has three sets of guy wires. One set of three at the 40-foot interface between the main sections, and another set at the top.

Imagine the tower lying with one flat side of its triangle on the ground, and one point of its triangle facing the sky and all the guy wires attached and just lying there. I took the top guy wire on the side facing up, strung it across a sort of saddle at the mid-point interface and attached it to a seven-and-a-half-ton mechanical winch that you tighten by hand. Then I attached the winch to the bottom of the tower and cinched it up till I saw the top lift slightly off the ground. That made the 76-foot tower rigid. If I hadn't done that, any attempt to lift it would have just snapped it in half at its weakest point.

We installed what's called a roving snatch block (a pulley with a hook that travels freely on a cable) on a strong cable that was strung high up between two strong oaks. Then we hooked another pulley onto that snatch block and strung the 20-ton winch cable through it from the back of our D4 Caterpillar dozer. Then we took the winch able back to the tower and hooked it on the mid-point interface.

This is tough to explain, but we used a high lift and a backhoe to initiate the lift before we engaged the Cat's winch. I tried lifting it with one highlift and my back wheels promptly lifted off the ground. It was too heavy. So we used the backhoe too. My cousin Boo was on the Cat and he engaged the winch and up it went. It was a tense moment. So many things could have gone wrong, but it all went right.

There are several other ways to erect towers using gin poles, for example, but this one worked for us. I'm getting too old and tired and nerved-out to climb it anymore, so in the last year I thought to put up two more towers close to the first. Then I'll have a bigger triangle inside of which I can install a crude elevator and on top of which I can build a platform and put my two other windmills that are just sitting doing nothing.

A Windmill Near-Death Experience

I really am a cautious guy, but I tend to go at life like a mildly raging warrior at times. More than one relative of mine has said to me, "I have neither seen nor heard of any person who has sustained more blunt force ass-ripping, life-threatening traumas than you, Teddy." If I wrote the story of my life it would consist mainly of a very long list of events that would probably make you wince.

It happened that there was a pine tree close to the house whose root wad had torn loose on one side. It threatened to fall on the house and take out a set of guy wires in the next strong wind. When winds would start up, I took to backing a piece of heavy equipment on that side of the root wad for support.

It was around 4 pm, 15 degrees and falling fast, and there came such a winter blast that it tore roofs off of buildings not far from here. I couldn't get any tractor started and the tree was swaying so much you couldn't even look at it without your knees feeling like buckling.

I had no choice but to climb it while it was swaying and cut the top 25 feet off so the wind would lose its leverage. Unless you were there, you can't imagine what that was like. When I was done with the tree I climbed back down frozen, nerves shot, and I doubt I could have crushed a piece of toilet paper in my hands. I walked over to the windmill to check the mechanical brake, decided to maybe give it another notch just to be sure – and the cable broke. I watched a wave in the cable travel 76 feet up the tower and unhook itself from the brake rod that sticks out the bottom of the windmill itself. By now it was really getting dark and the released windmill was going so fast and out of control I thought its blades were just gonna shatter.

The winds were probably 50 mph, plus or minus, with occasional gusts of I don't know what speed. I grabbed the cable that had since fallen to the ground and headed up the tower. I had to feed the cable up the center as I climbed and when I got near the top I was faced with the fact that there was an out-of-control saw blade spinning so fast you couldn't see it, and it was quickly and erratically changing directions.

I was up there close to that blade for 15 or 20 minutes trying to get up enough nerve to chance a sprint up the last few rungs and grab the brake rod before the wind changed directions. If my timing had been off and the wind kicked it around, my friend Arthur standing below would have had a nice shower of flesh, bones, blood and windmill blade shards.

I was never so close to suicide in my life. I simply couldn't judge my grip. I was convinced I couldn't possibly hold on. My arms and hands were so exhausted they felt like they were full of Novocain instead of blood. I near convinced myself I couldn't possibly make it. My life began to flash before me and everything I thought was worth living for became transparent and ghostlike. I was within half a hairsbreadth of just letting myself fall. I looked down at a certain grape arbor post thinking if I land on that I won't survive the fall. I must have blacked out because somehow I found myself on the ground again and I can't say how I got there.

What I do know is that I had killed the nerves in my front teeth that night and I had initial stage frostbite on my hands.

My nervous system was so traumatized that the next day when I was in the forest I suddenly collapsed flat on the ground in a state of temporary paralysis. It happened again the day after that. See why I want an elevator?

The windmill I used for years worked like those old bicycle generators that flipped up to spin against your tire. As you peddled, it lit up your driving light. Now they install magnets on the wheel and there is no real friction, bearings or armature. I could fix just about anything that broke on my old windmill. My new windmill is magnetic and electronic and I can't fix a damn thing on it if it breaks down. What's nice is the new windmill is self-regulating with its own internal brake and charge control – a huge improvement over the old one.

Solar Power

The decision to use solar power was a no-brainer for us. We started out with three cheap solar panels I got at the flea market, hooked up to three car batteries in series. That let us use the Electrolux vacuum and a few kitchen appliances. When two of those panels died, we upgraded to three 75-watt top-of-the-line solar panels and the equivalent number of batteries, the same type and number that run a golf cart. We added three more 75-watt panels when our windmill was down for close to a year and a half, and that got us by all year round. Even if it's a snowy day in winter, the sun will still produce a lot of amps. Keeping the panels snow-free is a minor task.

I also have a collage set of miscellaneous panels I picked up

Our windmill tower

Battery banks   **A solar panel array**

White white lightning 190 proof ethanol alcohol
(Swedish Primus alcohol stove, flea market price: $1)

at the flea market. They're all wired together to trickle charge a larger bank of batteries or to directly charge something like a car battery. This total number of panels seems more than adequate for our conservative needs. I can separate the six panels into three and three, and with the miscellaneous panels I have three charge sources. I can combine any two or direct them all toward one effort. That's thanks to the obsolete control panel Dad picked up out of his company's garbage. I can also introduce the windmill into the same club.

I do have to mechanically angle them to the sun, which needs to be done four times a year. Here's one of my dreams for fine-tuning that function: If I had unlimited energy and time, I have in mind something inspired by surface-to-air gun turrets, or the ones in the old bomber planes where you had total control of where your seat would point. Only, instead of pointing a machine gun I'd be turning the seat cranks to sight-in the direct sun. When I'd see a light bull's eye on the mirror target board in front of me I'd know the panels are in the most efficient pose, both latitude and longitude. I have the tower for it and some of the mechanics, but I don't know if my sun turret will ever pull a low enough number on The Stone Camp's necessity draft lottery.

A useful tip: I discovered a great way to make a frame for a solar array. It turns out that U-shaped stop sign posts work beautifully to weld up your own frame. That's a money saver! Their many holes happen to line up with the mounts for both my brands, so there's a good chance they'll work for most panels. Some good news is that the price of solar cells has been steadily coming down.

White White Lightning: Ethanol

You can't drink 190 proof ethanol, but there's a lot you can use it for besides as a disinfectant. We're using it to cook with now and I've heard there's such a thing as alcohol lanterns. I hope to master a Briggs and Stratton conversion to alcohol, and also two or three of my tractors. My main target is my 1960 Jeep FC170 one-ton truck with three PTO's (power take-offs). It's slated to be the last running vehicle, and the ultimate multi-purpose unit. When it is no longer feasible to keep all these tractors, trucks and vehicles running, and gasoline's like gold, this alcohol-fueled FC170 Jeep will be equipped with its own electric plant, hydraulic system and a category one 3-point hitch PTO, just like on a farm tractor. Germany had such a vehicle, called a Unimog (One-use). You plow the fields and then drive it to church on Sunday. Ironically, the Unimog looks very much like an FC Jeep.

I hope to put a 2-way dump bed on mine to dump off the back and the right side as well, and a snowplow mount. All of my years of experience building vehicles and doing mechanics will reach fruition in this one vehicle. It will also run the saw-mill, stone crusher, wood chipper, large welding alternator and a three-point hitch backhoe, if need be. You might call it a tri-fuel, since it'll run on gasoline and wood gas as well. It's gonna happen, sooner than later. Anyone who knows me well and has viewed some of my past creations would bank on it.

We just ran off our first 190 proof in the Charles 803 ethanol still, designed by the late Robert Warren. He's a guy from England who spent a good portion of his life experimenting with refractory column stills. I can't remember how many prototypes he built but there were many. What a cool man he was. We bought the blueprints from him for $26 and he'd email from time to time to see how we were doing. My buddy Drewcilla and I assembled the unit down at Dad's garage. He's a retired merchant marine who worked for BP. His is real name is Drew. He calls me Tedweena. We bonded in first grade and vowed never to mature. As you might guess, we kept that vow.

The still has 600 glass marbles inside its columns. I'm not going to get into describing how it works because it's complicated and I don't feel I have the right. I believe his daughter runs the business now and you can get info online. The unit looks like an outhouse from the outside. One thing that bothered me in the years of planning was wasted heat. I was going to be bringing close to 50 gallons of real rotgut wine (fermented waste sugar solution from an industrial bakery) to a boil, keeping it there till all the alcohol was stripped out of it.

Because the boiler is converted from a hot water heating system it has an inner coil used to transfer heat. I could use this coil for what's called a closed loop system, which means I could send antifreeze, oil or most any cold liquid through the coil, literally suck the heat out of that 50 gallons and transfer it somewhere else via a small inline pump. It basically means I'd transfer the heat from one stationary liquid to another mobile liquid. That's one of the options I had for transferring heat to the big compost toilet that's in the making (see Chapter 11).

I discovered another practical use for the still, by chance. Just like my eyes falling on the back window of the Subaru Justy (when I had that revelation about using its heat energy for my compost toilet), they fell on some old corn dryers I have. A corn dryer is like a big metal pizza box. It's sealed except for a tiny opening in one corner. You fill it with water, set it on top of the wood stove and spread the corn on it that you just cut off fresh from the garden. The 212° dry heat dries the corn evenly without scorching it. BINGO! The still now doubles as a food dryer, thus the built-in venting to direct the heat flow to the dryer trays and out the front top.

A cautionary tale

We just ran off our first batch of 190 proof a couple weeks ago. The still amazed us. It spit pure 190 out of its designated spout – and then it just stopped producing. If you don't think I live an exciting life, let me tell you about that day.

I didn't want to fire up an entire 50 gallons to test the still and make its adjustments. So we made a smaller boiler made out of a stainless half-keg and used propane to heat it. It sat on its side and there's a filler cap where the bung plug is (also mid-point on the side). That's about a 2-inch hole, so we reduced it down to 5/8-inch so it could be hooked to the steam line (a 5/8" radiator hose). It's through that line that the water steam and alcohol vapor go to the still to be processed.

There's another spout that spews out a "low proof" liquid into a plastic jug and then you just keep adding that to the next batch. Since one jug was full and the boiler cap so easy to pop off, I said to Dad, "You have gloves on, pop that off so I can pour this in now. Why keep it till later?"

The low proof is about the same alcohol content as wine, and wine isn't flammable, so it took us several days to realize that if you pour wine over a hot surface the pure alcohol vapors steam off first, before the water. As I was pouring the low-proof into the 2-inch hole I spilled a little and it ran down the side of the keg to the boiler's temporary propane heating flame underneath. Next thing you know, up comes this blue flame to the steam vent. Next thing you know, the alcohol vapors ignited. Up the side comes this blue flame to the steam vent. It in turn ignited the alcohol vapors coming out of the still, and a roaring blue ball of intense flame is suspended in front of my face like a planet suspended in space.

Then it reached for and ignited the low-proof jug whose liquid was hot because it had just come from being condensed steam. That caught my hands and forearms on fire and I let go of the jug, which somehow ended up drenching my dad. Then that ball of fire aimed straight at my dad and shot at him like a cannonball. I looked at him and he was completely engulfed in blue flame head to toe.

I remember him trying to part it in front of his face so he could catch a breath of air. I was opposite Dad on the other side of the still. I watched Mark and Sebastian trying to put out the fire and it wasn't working. Sebastian yelled, "Drop and roll!" Dad went down and got his torso out, but the heavy cotton jeans – the perfect wick – just wouldn't stop burning. I finally put myself out and got to him and started beating on his legs, accidentally punching him in the you-know-what.

We were all laughing like hell from the moment we saw the

first flame, laughed the whole time it happened and were still laughing when we walked into the house.

Dad had on a polar fleece jacket that afterwards decomposed like old parchment, and a hat that covered his ears. All that got singed was what Mom called his "devils eyebrow" that often stuck up like a horn, especially when he was ornery. After that happened, a noticeable change came over him. He had a short surge of zest for life and as God is my witness he called just minutes ago and asked, "Are you running the still today?" I said, "No, why?" He said, "Well, I looked in the mirror this morning and that damn devil's eyebrow is growing back."

Converting a battery charger to alcohol

I'm close to converted my battery charger extreme to run on alcohol instead of gasoline. I'll have two tanks, a big one for ethanol and a little one for gasoline. To postpone having to build a pre-heater for the ethanol, I've got a workaround: I'll start it on gas, let it warm up a bit and then switch it to ethanol. I power this 12-volt 65-amp charger with the drive train from a 12 h.p. Massey Ferguson garden tractor. The tractor's been stripped down to frame, engine, battery mount and electric starter. Instead of driving wheels, it just sits and drives an alternator. I built my charger two years ago, and I advise anybody who lives this way to have one.

This is an emergency charger you can build from any single-cylinder gasoline engine, a 65-amp car alternator and a control box with a huge rheostat. The rheostat lets you control the charge instead of a regulator or transistors. With the turn of a handle you can throw as much power into your batteries as you want and charge them up fast. They say you can use a 5 h.p. engine, but even on this 12 h.p. engine, when you flip the charge switch, man does the motor load down. You can actually feel it laboring to produce electrons. There's a company that assembles and sells the control box complete, but they're easy to build if you understand them and have a schematic. I've used maybe a total of three gallons of gasoline so far in two years.

Making alcohol from tree sap

Kathy and I tap our red maple trees and make our own syrup, as described in Chapter 9. Besides making the best-tasting syrup you've ever tasted, I've got another use for the sap: alcohol. If and when I'm reduced to making alcohol from tree sap, I will have achieved the ultimate in raw sustainability. Being that I make such an effort to care for and tend the forest's strength and equilibrium, you might call it a true symbiotic relationship. Once the sap is collected in late winter tapping season I need only boil out about half the water to get a 20% sugar solution. Actual table syrup is boiled much further down and maple sugar takes all the water out. But I must also ferment it immediately so it doesn't spoil. That means the fermenting barrels must be set to working in a heated area. It's possible to heat the fermenting barrels from the radiance of the syrup boilers themselves. I have no need to use maple sap for ethanol at the moment, and probably won't for many years – the reason being that I currently have a huge supply of waste sugar from a factory bakery nearby. It's enough to supply me with necessary fermentation stock for a very long time.

Thermoelectric

In the Refrigeration chapter I talk about 12-volt Peltier crystal units that can be made to produce power from either methane or wood smoke. No need to repeat the information here.

Methane

In Chapter 11 I called methane one of nature's miracle energy sources. Turning human and animal waste into a power source is an example of recycling at its best. In the black water section of that chapter I introduced my methane digester. I'm collecting methane gas as you read this. I haven't calculated how many cubic feet I have in storage yet, but the digester and collector are finished and working.

Methane is what's slated ultimately to run our propane refrigerator. If the need presents itself, I also have a 2KW AC generator that will run on it. At the moment, the generator is mounted in my electric shop under the workbench. Being that I'm driven by necessity, putting the methane generator online keeps getting shoved down the project list. But any day that could change. I have my eye on multiple uses for our methane. Its first use will no doubt be a demonstration of thermoelectricity. About the methane generator – I'm thinking I'll take it down and install it at my dad's on propane, because it came with the electronic control system to start automatically if the grid shuts down. I have no need of that, he does. I can also wood-gas any of these generator systems, if need be. That's a power source near and dear to my heart.

Outbuilding housing methane storage tanks

Close-up of methane storage tanks

4 of the 6 wood gasifier subunits

Wood Gasification

June 22, 7:23 pm. The old Oliver tractor roared to life. So why did I jump up on the seat, dance an Irish jig and scream war whoops like I just won the big lottery? The engine was running on wood smoke! No fossil fuel required.

They call it wood gasification. VW developed the process in the late thirties. Hitler used it during WW2 because he got cut off from gas and diesel. Most impressive is the fact that 95% of the gas/diesel motors in German-occupied Denmark ran off wood smoke. At the same time, neutral Sweden was running 40% of its cars and trucks on wood or charcoal, and there were millions of wood gas generators in use all over Asia. Even more impressive is the fact that today almost nobody knows about it.

Except for a $26 butterfly valve, we (the three M's, Mark Matt and myself) built our gasification unit from discarded junk: an old 100-pound propane tank, a hot water tank, some chains, a chunk of ¼-inch plate stainless steel, a pressurized water tank cut in two to make both filters, a small 12-volt heater fan, a manhole heat exchanger, two steel tire rims, a bunch of inch-and-a-half and two-inch pipe and various dimensional chunks of steel.

Our wood gasifier has seven subunits: a somewhat complex combustion chamber, two cooler-condensers, two smoke filters (one a primary centrifugal and the other a secondary particulate filter), a 12-volt starter fan made out of a heater blower, and a simple homemade carburetor. Of the cooler condensers, one's an optional supercharger. Our supercharger is made out of a huge Schramm radiator with a giant Volvo cooling fan. When you send the smoke through it and hit the fan switch, it strips out so much moisture it sounds like a waterfall descending inside the unit.

We had three sets of blueprints – a crude, a medium and a refined. One actually came from FEMA (crude), but I don't know if it's still available; one was featured in Mother Earth News (somewhat refined), and the third one my cousin Boo had (really sophisticated and refined).

FEMA's booklet is called "Wood Gasification in the Event of Petroleum Shortage." It's a throwaway unit that you can literally put together in a day. You need a 30-gallon drum can, a 16-gallon garbage can with lid, a 5- or 7-gallon paint can, a stainless steel kitchen colander, a cast iron skillet, a small sack of waterproof paint for cement pools (powder form) and various other common smaller items you can find lying around. The picture on the front of the pamphlet has a John Deere tractor plowing a field with this unit hanging on the front.

The Mother Earth News unit was set in the back of a Chevy pickup. They drove this pickup coast-to-coast, stopping along back-forested roads to cut limbs and at woodshops to scrounge for scrap off-cuts. They carried an electric chain saw with them – I think it was 12-volt DC or maybe 12-volt converted to 110-volt AC. Either way you could use the truck battery to power it.

Boo's unit is called the Pegusus. It's damned sophisticated and you pretty much need a machine or metal fabrication shop to build it. His dad (Uncle Bob) first saw a wood gasifier in 1946 when he was in the army. Just after the war he was stationed in Japan. He said every morning from his balcony he could see an old Japanese taxi driver hand cranking a blacksmith blower on back of his 1932 Chevy coupe. This guy ran his taxi service on wood smoke.

The 3M's studied the plans for each of these units twice in order to fully comprehend the process. Then we assembled ours, which is somewhat unique. Mother Earth News said you could probably throw one together for between $300 and $350. Aside from the $26 valve, we only had a welding rod and electricity in ours. A bit later I actually found one of these valves helping my buddy Nathan clear out his basement.

The flame of a wood fire is itself burning gas, so the idea is to extract that gas in its purest, driest form. Roughly 22 pounds of wood equals a gallon of gasoline. I'm not sure what that is in pounds of liquid propane. The whole process is just as if you took total control of your campfire. You light it but stall flame ignition by depriving it of O2. Then you control, manage and proportion the unburned gasses to ignite in the engine's cylinders instead of using it to cook wieners. The ignition-managed campfire feeds the combustion cycle that's harnessed to turn your wheels.

You have to refine the wood gas. First, you burn it starved of air and then send the smoldering smoke over a heap of glowing embers without its bursting into flame. That induces a chemical change known as pyrolisis. The engine's efficiency is relative to the amount of moisture and particulate you get out of the unburned smoke, and also how cool you can get the gas before it combusts.

Some say it's the cleanest form of combustion there is. What's not pre-filtered is cleanly incinerated when the piston fires. Its exhaust is something like the smokeless fire that the Indians knew how to build. To expand on the campfire analogy, think about waking up and finding your campfire's gone out. You frantically sift through the ashes and find a few hot coals and then you scramble for some real dry tinder. Then you heap the finest tinder on those coals and start blowing for your life or maybe just your coffee and breakfast. If you're lucky it starts to smoke. Then it smokes more and more until it's billowing. Then in one flash it bursts into bright yellow flame.

A wood gasifier brings the campfire to its billowing stage but stops it from bursting into flame by controlling the air intake. Then it processes the flammable gasses for the internal combustion that sends you down the road. Currently, our wood-gasified Oliver is slated to power the huge things. It can power the 7KW alternator I use for welding, but my buddy Mark wants to build a scaled-down wood gasifier unit to run an alternator unit similar to my 12 h.p. battery charger. We've got big plans for wood gasification!

The Oliver

The old Oliver 66 is a tricycle. That means its two front wheels are close to touching each other for cultivating rows (thus "row-cropper"). They say they're dangerous in the woods because they tip easily, but I've had way more hair-raisers with my low-rider Ford tractors, the 8Ns, the 800, the 801 and the Dexta diesel. The Oliver's front tires are spread as wide apart as the back tires and that makes them way more stable. However, I've had every one of them up on two wheels more times than I'd like to admit.

That's because I push them right to their stability edge on steep hills and rocky terrain.

I seem to be able to weave the Oliver in and around trees and rocks much easier than any of the Fords – you can turn the front wheels 90 degrees sideways, lock one back brake and turn it instantly left and right. This huge tractor can also sit there and easily spin itself in circles around the locked wheel.

So imagine that here's this old tractor and on the back is its PTO-driven wood chipper that can hook onto it. Imagine that instead pouring in red cans of gasoline, this tractor goes out in the forest from time to time chipping up next month's fuel supply from dead limbs and blowing them into the trailer it pulls behind it. It is of itself making its own fuel. It has achieved self-reliance. It's the epitome of raw sustainability and symbiosis with the forest. It's not looking to "father petrol" anymore to run the sawmill, the stone-crusher or pull the heavy trailer loads of winter wood out of the forest.

Any of my big tractors (and I'm never quite sure how many I have) are capable of doing many tasks. They can all run on my 7KW alternator I use for welding, which could power a small hospital. One thing I hope the tractors will do in the future is to pay my dad's electric bill, or at least reimburse him if I suck power off his meter doing projects in his shops.

Dad's place is on grid, as I said. He has an electric meter. Both the wood and mechanics shop are at his place. Eventually I'd like to bring one of the alternative fuel tractors down (wood gas, biodiesel or alcohol), back up to his meter and plug my big alternator into the grid. Then every two months, the day before the guy comes to read it for billing, I'd send Dad's meter spinning backward at warp speed till it hit zero. Up to zero you get dollar for dollar. If you sell them more than what you use they pay you much less. What else did you expect?

Having experienced the epiphany of building a wood gasification unit and seeing it run, my eyes are on forest fires, especially the western fires. The dead limbs and underbrush that cause the fires is the stuff that's running the old Oliver tractor. Knowing what I know about wood gasification, I can't even imagine how much potential electric power just goes up in smoke when a forest fire goes aggressive. But we'll keep on having disastrous forest fires until our national forestry practices undergo a drastic change.

This is not the place for me to take off on government's forestry practices, but you can probably guess that I have some very strong feelings about it. At the end of the book I'll tell you what I know about these practices, what needs to be changed to restore equilibrium to our forests – and how the only solution is a true understanding of stewardship. Imagine one day seeing your local gas station dispensing prepared wood pellets along with alcohol and bio-fuels. I have a dream.

The wood-gas-powered Oliver

13

Eight Small DIY Projects

"All you need is..."

1

BIODEGRADABLE SEEDLING MARKER

Skill level: minimal
Cost: 0

This is a tiny "get you in the mood" idea I came up with for Kathy when she needed to mark her seedlings. It's a nice project for children who want to help out in the garden.

What you need:
- matchbook cover (one cover makes two markers)
- incense stick
- fine tip Sharpie pen (waterproof ink)

How to do the project:
1. Snip off the striker plate and cut the matchbook's length in half.
2. Write the name of the plant on the blank side of one of the halves.
3. Punch two holes in the matchbook, top and bottom. (I like to use an old ice pick, but a nail would work)
4. Lace the incense stick through the holes and plant your little flag in the flat with the seeds.

2

PLASTIC BALL TRAP FOR FRUIT TREE PESTS

skill level: minimal
cost: $6+

Many insect pests are attracted to form as well as color, so they see this big red ball and fly to it to take a bite or lay their larvae. You can buy them at Toys "R" Us, but why spend that kind of money? I find these balls at the flea market. I figured out I could just spray paint any color ball red. The only thing you have to buy is a can or two of Tanglefoot, a sticky substance that you brush on. The insects fly onto the ball and stay.

What you need:
- a 6" ball (and red spray paint, if needed)
- old wire clothes hanger
- metal snips
- pliers for bending the wire
- a propane torch to heat the end of the wire
- Tanglefoot (comes with a brush)

How to do the project:
1. Spray the ball with red paint if needed. Let it dry.
2. Cut a foot or more section of hanger, heat the end with the torch and pierce the ball at its axis, straight through the middle, until the wire protrudes a few inches out the other side.
3. Make a 90-degree bend on that short piece so it won't pull back through. That will be the bottom. For the 8 or more inches that stick out the top, bend that end of the wire into a hook.
4. Paint it up with Tanglefoot and you've got your insect trap.
5. Hang 3 to 5 per tree.

Testimonial: We just had a hailstorm, and yes, it was the size of golf balls. All but one of my commercial-bought ones smashed to pieces, but not the homemade ones.

Seedling markers

Chapel hinge

Apple mill, showing bike sprocket drive and chipper

Apple mill with wooden hopper in place

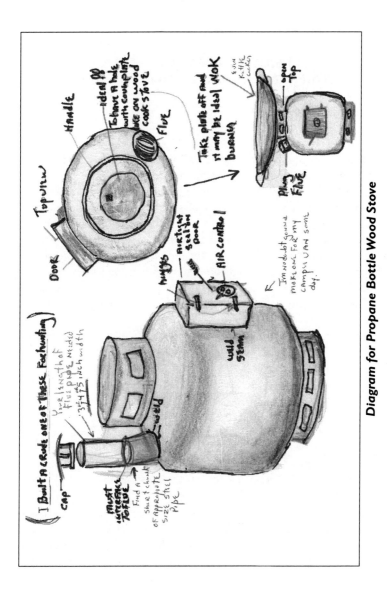

(I Built a Crude one of These for hunting)

Cap

Your length of flue pipe needed
3&1/2 inch width

MUST WEATHER TOP FLUE

Find a shut chunk of appropriate size steel pipe

Burner

Welded Seam

AIR control

Hinges

Airtight Seal on Door

I'm nodulot sound
Makiem for my
camper van some
day.

Top view

Door

Handle

Ideal Ø

Exhaust Ø hole
with convenplant

like an wood
cook stove

Flue

Take plate off and
it may be ideal WOK
burner

Extra
Kettle
cooker

Open
Top

Plug
Flue

Diagram for Propane Bottle Wood Stove

205

3

A LEAK-PROOF VALVE FOR A
RAINWATER COLLECTION BARREL

Skill level: Handyman
Cost: $5-$10

I have a commercial biofilter for a small fish pond. Every piece of it is custom-made, which accounts for the high price you'd have to pay for a new one. The biofilter is contained in a designer 4-gallon plastic jug. One part of the filter is so similar to the scrubbing part of a kitchen floor scrubber you'd mistake it for one. The whole unit is filled with special plastic shapes that I feel function no better or worse than an assortment of plastic bottle caps would. The only thing that's complex is the plumbing. Having understood the design of the pond filter, this next handy how-to technique lets me build one of any size. Which gets me to: plumbing plastic barrels together for a rainwater collection system.

Plumbing many barrels together makes them all fill up the same rate. This project creates a leak-proof fitting. (It also works for installing valves like a garden spigot.)

What you need:
- an old inner tube (for cutting out 2 gaskets)
- 2 steel washers (preferably galvanized) I.D. (inner dimension), $7/8$"
- 2 electrical conduit nuts
- an appropriate size and length of pipe (nipple). I use $1/2$" pipe which is O.D. (outer dimension) thickness $7/8$", but $3/4$" and even 1" will work.

To figure the length, set the barrels exactly where you want them to sit, measure between them and add an inch or two. Make sure both ends are threaded to match your conduit nuts. The pipe comes in galvanized, plastic, brass and steel – or you can sweat (solder) one up with copper fittings as well. I prefer plastic, but never steel.

How to do the project:

1. Drill the ⅞" holes on the sides of the barrels about 1½" off the bottom, or cut them carefully by hand with an X-ACTO knife. I use a professional hole punch which is like a glorified beefed-up paper punch. It's made to punch though thin steel.

2. With scissors or X-ACTO knife cut the ⅞" I.D. rubber gaskets from the inner tube. The center hole should be as close to a round ⅞" as possible.

3. Assemble the pipe, gaskets, washers and nuts in this order: nut-washer-gasket. Make sure the barrel hole is in the middle, then gasket-washer-nut. Then tighten one of the conduit nuts while holding the other fast. You can do that with two common pliers or channel lock pliers. No need to go too tight. Depending how deep the plastic drum is, it may take two people to tighten the conduit nuts. That can be solved using vice grips on one side.

4

CHAPEL HINGES

Skill level: Handyman – some knowledge of welding and blacksmithing
Cost: I may have at most $15 in these

This is an example of what you can do with things you find at the flea market. I do blacksmithing, but to make a set of hinges like these from scratch would put a hole in the ozone layer above my head. These babies I assembled are quite nice. I only fired the forge to do a wee bit of straightening. The main four bodies are made from old-fashioned hay hooks and the filigree from some old shutter fixtures, cut in half. I just welded them together in the design I decided on.

5

APPLE MILL

Skill level: handyman – some knowledge of welding
Cost: for me, no cost at all, except for a welding rod (but if
you have to buy new pillow blocks and all new metal, it
could total upwards of $175)

I give most of the design credit for this unit to my buddy Cal. If you've got the metalworking skills to build this you no doubt have the concept skills to envision it. It's bike-pedal driven. The grinder is just a chunk of 6" pipe with little 1" x ½" pieces cut from a length of bar stock that's 1" wide and ⅛" thick. The flywheel can be any heavy, round disc-like thing. Mine is a huge pulley from a ski rope tow lift.

We threw this one together in two days' spare time. We welded up a sturdy frame from random chunks of steel, considering work height and the need for a shelf underneath for the mash-collecting bucket. Then we took an old bicycle and stripped a pedal mechanism with a 7" sprocket and a 2½" wheel sprocket. We originally had a handle welded on the big flywheel and decided it was too dangerous and we cut it off.

What you need:

Parts for the chopper and drive

- a round axle or steel shaft ¾" thick by 21" long
- a 7" long chunk of 6" steel pipe. Ends must be cut somewhat perfect or milled to an even face.
- 2 flat 6" washers
- 2 washers (¾" I.D.), if needed
- 2 pillow blocks (¾") These are the axle bearings upon which everything spins
- As many chunks of 1" wide by ⅛" bar stock (flat bar) cut ½" to ⅝" long, as you need to go around the 6" pipe. These are the chopper teeth.

How to do the project (the chopper and drive):

1. Weld the 2 big flat washers to the ends of the 6" pipe, like you're capping them.

2. For the chopper teeth: Weld the cut pieces of bar stock to the 6" pipe, only on the leeward side of the spin, the side that doesn't do the chopping. Make the rows look like lines of soldiers: one 5-across row next to a 4-across row. Make the rows about 2" apart the whole way around the 6" pipe. We cut these pieces with our electric band saw but a 4" grinder with a metal cutting wafer works quicker. You can also use a hacksaw.

3. After they're all welded on, slide the whole chopper assembly onto the ¾" axle. The 6" washers you found probably don't have exact ¾" holes in them. They're probably bigger, so they'll wobble up and down. The trick here is to find 2 tight-fitting ¾" I.D. washers and slide one on from each side. Now the challenge lies in centering the whole chopper so that it turns smoothly with the axle. No wobbling. Once you get it there, you simply weld the washers together first, and then weld it fast to the axle via the washers.

4. On one end of the axle just past the outside of the pillow block, fix and balance your heavy flywheel however way you see fit. On the other end you must center and weld the smaller $2^{3}/8$" wheel sprocket. In order from left: welded sprocket, 1st pillow block, left side of chopper, right side, 2nd pillow block and flywheel. At this point the pillow blocks can still be slid side to side on the axle.

5. On the top surface of the frame you designed, you should be looking down on a 2-dimensional picture frame, a rectangle whose sides have some flat steel surface. All you have to do is set your entire chopper axle on it and center one pillow block on either side of the frame. Now give it a little test spin!

6. Center the 6" chopper in the narrow of that rectangle, but a little to one side of the length of it because you need room for the pedal mechanism. Center everything as best you can, using your eye and a ruler and then give it a spin to make sure the pillow block bearings are centered free of resistance.

7. The pillow blocks usually have two holes to mount them. Mark the holes, drill them and bolt them to the frame.

8. Cut the inner pedal from the bike drive, grab the chain and slip it on both sprockets and do some eyeballing as to where you need to mount the pedal mechanism. Do it preferably with some kind of length-adjusting mechanism. I'll leave that entirely up to you – you can even use wood.

9. The hopper/feeder (shown on p. 204): The hopper/feeder is made from sassafras wood. It's pretty simple to build. Only remember, it's a square funnel made to slip down over the chopper unit like a glove, but it doesn't touch or rest on moving parts. The bottom, of course, empties into the mash bucket. We fill the mash bucket three times and then it's off to the cider press.

6

WASHING MACHINE BOILER

Skill level: handyman
Cost: my cost – nothing; for you, no more than 30 bucks –
    if you can find a stainless tub in a scrap yard

This is one of my favorites anybody can build who's handy. All you need is one of these common washing machine tubs. The lid is one of those old antique aluminum disc sleds. The washing machine tub fits perfectly inside a cut-off 55-gallon drum. It even has a lip around the outside that seals and holds the tub into the drum, so the drum is a self-contained, extremely safe, lightweight portable fireplace that also holds, suppports and suspends the tub on top of the fire. This is a simple project with infinite uses. I can whip one out in 20 minutes without rushing. I've made syrup in these and cooked corn and boiled wine- and alcohol-making solutions. If you're canning big time, you can cold and hot pack around 22 quarts at once in this thing.

What you need:
- a common 55-gallon steel drum
- a stainless washing machine tub
- any size stove pipe 90
- a pop rivet gun and rivets
- 4- or 5-inch round piece of stainless steel

How to do the project:
1. There are about five or six ways to do the three cuts that have to be made on the steel drum. I prefer the air hammer with a cutting tip. You can torch it out with acetylene, use a 4" grinder, find someone with a plasma cutter or just use a saber saw with a metal cutting blade (remember not to use the #3 oscillator setting – you want the #1 setting).
2. First cut the barrel in half, then cut the little half moon doorway for feeding the fire. And last, cut the round stove pipe hole opposite the door, 3 or so inches from the top.
3. The stove pipe 90 should slide in that hole and can be pop riveted on by cutting ears (small 1" flaps) that bend out 90 degrees.

7

PROPANE BOTTLE WOOD STOVE

Skill level: handyman
Cost for the heater itself : cheap (if you're a patient scrounger) – welding rod, propane tank and various scrap pieces of steel. Stove pipe and elbows are the biggest expense – $100 or so, as a conservative estimate.

I just love this idea. I built a crude one for Dad to use at his hunting stand. Uninspected propane bottles are as common as dirt and hard to get rid of. I see them floating down rivers. I think you could manufacture and market an emergency heater unit kit using this idea. If and when

I build a deluxe one it'll go in my camper van. I've already picked up a revolving chimney cap (like from a caboose). It has a shark fin that turns it and adjusts for wind direction so you get no downdraft.

What you need for a complete emergency packet:

- I propane bottle
- plywood, sized to fit a window, through which the exhaust from the chimney stove pipe exits to the outside
- a flat piece of metal sheeting about the thickness of a car fender, with a 5" hole cut out of the middle
- sufficient 5" elbows and stove pipe to "do the smoke run" from stove to the atmosphere. This will vary, but won't need to pass code because it's for an emergency.

How to do the project:

1. Remove or simply open any window that is to become the chimney exit and measure to replace it with plywood.
2. Cut a 12" by 12" hole in the plywood and center it with the 5" hole in the metal sheet.
3. Screw or bolt the metal to the plywood. This will keep the hot stove pipe from igniting the plywood.
4. Place and secure plywood into window opening and fasten it with screws.
5. Set the stove on a makeshift fireproof hearth (a big flat stone).
6. Run the 5" stove pipe and elbows from the stove through the window and out into the atmosphere. All stove pipe has a crimped end – always place crimped ends toward the stove, or else you'll be plagued with seeping liquid creosote at every joint. Placed correctly, the creosote runs "funnel-like" back into the fire.
7. Secure your stove pipe run with whatever braces you think you may need. You're dealing with fire, so keep Teddy's overkill in mind.
8. Set a fire with kindling and light as you would a wood stove. Let it get going hot and then shut the door and adjust the air vent to match the heat you want it to radiate.

I've made a sketch of a more refined idea. With a good door gasket and air control one should burn for many hours. They make cast iron interfaces for masonry chimneys. I use them on all the wood stoves I built, to interface with the stove pipe. They look like Abe Lincoln's top hat with all but two inches of the top cut off. If you're into making this stove into a portable heat source for wok or kettle I'd forget the exhaust in the sketch design and take it right out the top of the propane tank with one of these cast iron pieces. You can weld this cast piece to the steel tank with special welding rod but it will crack and fissure because cast and steel expand at different rates. So imagine cutting the "hat" hole (minus the brim of the hat) in the top of the propane tank. Open the stove door and shove it up through from the inside: Use fireproof gasket fiber or cement, drill through the brim and the tank and bolt them fast together (make the holes slightly bigger than the bolts to allow for the expansion difference). Keep in mind this is a temporary emergency heating unit built with safety in mind but not building code.

8

STOVETOP FOOD DRYER

Skill level: low
Cost: a few dollars or more, depending on where you find one

Once as common as dirt, these units have graduated to near antique status. I've picked up four or five of them for a couple of bucks each. They are ovens. Some even have thermometers on the doors. I put finer stainless mesh on the racks, elevate them off the wood stove a bit, leave the door open a crack and dry fruit in them.

What you need:
- 1 stovetop dryer
- fine stainless mesh, cut to size of the racks

How to do the project:

1. Place the fine mesh on the racks.
2. Elevate the dryer off the stove a bit.
3. Dry your fruit.

A "HOW-TO" TESTIMONY TO PATIENCE

We have a lovely marble candlestick that everyone raves about. It didn't start out to be a candlestick. It's another case of a project that made itself. I was at a yard sale and noticed a piece of decorative marble. I remember I said, "How much for this?" to the owner's wife. She said two or three bucks and her husband said, "What are you doing? My dad brought that home from Italy!" I offered him more and he said, "No that's okay, we're trying to get rid of stuff."

I got it home, looked at it and thought with some alteration it would make a nice candleholder. I didn't lift a finger, and five years later I'm walking through the flea market and see the small top piece of marble on a blanket of stuff that said 50 cents each. When I put the together it was a perfect fit and was just made for a taper candle. That epitomizes my approach to life: extreme patience.

Well worth the wait!

14

FAVORITE RECIPES FROM THE STONE CAMP KITCHEN

"...one Saturday morning we suddenly realized that the main ingredients in this hearty breakfast were grown, processed and cooked right here."

To give you a flavor of our diet, Kathy and I (mostly Kathy) have put together a few recipes that have given us and our guests pleasure, and that appear most often on our table.

Visitors enjoying a meal from The Stone Camp kitchen

Ted's Eccentric Smoothie
Makes 2 smoothies (about 10 ounces each)

We start each day with this one.

Ingredients
2½ cups of any combination of soy, rice or almond milk,
  diluted with a bit of spring water
1 heaping teaspoon each of the following dry ingredients:
  Bee pollen
  Powdered flax seed
  Powdered chia seed
  Nutritional yeast
  Soy lecithin
  Powdered brewer's yeast
  Powdered green drink
  Powdered pea protein

Additional dry ingredients:
  1 level teaspoon high quality cinnamon
  4 coral calcium capsules (I take them apart)

Generous dollop organic blackstrap molasses
1 organic banana
1 tablespoon nut butter (optional)

Directions
1. In a blender mix together the liquid and dry ingredients. Add
    the blackstrap molasses and the banana. Sometimes I'll add the
    nut butter if I'm cutting firewood or running the sawmill, just
    for the boost.

Our Epiphany Breakfast

**Corn pancakes
Tofu and soysage
Hash browns
Maple syrup**

We call this our epiphany breakfast because one Saturday morning we suddenly realized that the main ingredients in this hearty breakfast were grown, processed and cooked right here. The corn was a wonderful colorful Indian flint variety we grew one year, dried and ground into flour, the tofu and soysage were made from soybeans we grew, the syrup is our own and the hash brown potatoes were from the red variety we grow. The tofu and soysage recipe isn't ours, but you can find it in *"The Farm"* cookbook. We use our black soybeans and now we know that black soybeans make violet-colored tofu!

Here's Kathy's corn pancake recipe.

Corn pancakes
Makes eight 5-inch pancakes

Ingredients
   1⅓ cup cornmeal
   ⅔ cup spelt flour
   1 tablespoon baking powder
   ¼ teaspoon salt
   1⅔ cup soy milk
   1 teaspoon vanilla
   ⅓ cup flax seed mixture (Mix 1 heaping tablespoon ground
      flax seed with ¼ cup water and let sit 10-15 minutes until the
      consistency of raw egg.)

Directions

1. In a bowl, mix together cornmeal, flour, baking powder and salt. Add soymilk and vanilla and stir until combined. Fold in flax mixture.

2. Heat a griddle on medium-high heat, until a drop of water sizzles on it. Add a few drops of high heat oil. Spoon corn cake batter onto griddle, making cakes about 5 inches in diameter. Flip when top sides appear mostly dry, and cook for another minute or so, until cooked through.

Note: If we want to make our pancakes with only homegrown ingredients we could, by leaving out the spelt flour, baking powder, salt and vanilla. Enough maple syrup will make anything taste good!

Our Integrated Salad

We grow a number of lettuces. Besides lettuces, we grow a variety of other greens like kale, beet greens, Swiss chard and arugula.

The integrated aspect of our salads is the many wild greens we add from time to time: dandelion tenders (tender leaves), lamb's quarters, violet tenders, deer tongue (which I believe is better known as sorrel), and plantain tenders. The thing about wild greens in general is their super-nutritional value. The vitamin A in lamb's quarters is astronomical. Wild greens make common iceberg lettuce look like...well, for lack of a better word, a void, a place in which nothing dwells. In late spring and early summer our salads usually consist of any available lettuce that's mature enough to eat. We like to save a variety of seed from the previous year and then plant it in four-to-six-inch-wide rows in the garden.

To prepare one of our salads, we first wash the greens and put them in the salad spinner. Then we add washed tender greens from the yard, plus any other vegetables beginning to grow, like onions, kale, peas, etc. We like to include wild greens and edible flowers

We like honey mustard dressings, but we have no bees, so we play around instead with our own red maple syrup and add to it various mustards. Here's one of our favorite mustard dressings.

Maple Mustard Dressing
Makes 1¾ cups

Ingredients
¼ cup each of yellow prepared mustard, balsamic vinegar and
   maple syrup
⅔ cup olive oil
⅓ cup water

Directions
Combine ingredients in a quart jar. With the lid securely on, shake until well blended. For a different taste, use Dijon or any favorite mustard instead of yellow, and red wine vinegar instead of balsamic.

Beans and Torts
&
Vegan "Cheese" Dip

Beans and Torts is something I picked up in the Northwest during the early '70s. Some call it "hippie food" – I call it Superman's dinner delight, because the day after eating this particular protein combo our energy levels are through the roof. When I say that if driven to complete self-sustenance we'd revert to a simple Mexican peasant's diet, this would be a main meal that one could paint with an infinite variety of hues.

Whenever I see purslane sprouts that have "weeded up" in the garden I re-locate them in a central place. They grow into a plant with the taste and consistency of nopalitos (prickly pear cactus leaves that have been de-pricked), which are often added as filling in Mexican tortilla dishes. Greenbriar sprouts work too. We actually grew prickly pears one year. The first time we tried to cook them, though, I ended up getting the prickles on the roof of my mouth, my tongue and in my throat. They seemed to dissolve from the acid I secreted in my all-out mental panic.

Before we turned vegan we'd heap on the cheddar, along with the bean filling. Now we make a cheese substitute with nutritional yeast from a recipe we picked up at Penn State's Solidarity Conference where Kathy and I were both invited to speak. The tortillas (torts) are made with masa harina, a corn flour found in Mexican markets or some natural foods and grocery stores. The recipe and technique for making corn tortillas is usually found printed on the outside of the package. This is what works for us.

Homemade Tortillas
Makes 8 tortillas

Ingredients
2 cups masa harina
1¼ cup water, more or less
Dash salt

Directions

1. Place masa harina in a mixing bowl and add 1 cup water. Mix together, kneading with hands a few minutes to combine well. This dough ball should neither feel dry and crumbly nor sticky. Add small amounts of water as necessary to get the right consistency. Cover with moist towel to keep from drying out.

2. Break dough ball into eight equal pieces, rolling into small balls. Flatten these, then press in a tortilla press or use a rolling pin to flatten into desired thickness. We like the tortillas thinner than what the press makes so we then roll these between two pieces of plastic, then gently remove plastic.

3. Cook on a hot, dry griddle that has a sprinkle of salt on it to prevent sticking. When the tortilla can be easily lifted with a metal spatula, turn and cook a little on the other side. It should be dry but not crispy, still flexible, and may be a little browned in places. Practice makes perfect.

Tortilla Filling

We then fill the tortillas with any of the following, depending on time of year and available vegetables.

Ingredients

1 cup dry pinto beans (will yield about 2 cups cooked beans)
Salt to taste
Minced garlic, ground cumin, chili powder to taste (optional)

To cook dry beans:

Soak the cleaned and washed beans in water overnight (1 cup beans to 3 cups water). The next day bring to a boil and gently simmer until nearly tender. A quicker method is to cover the beans with water, bring to a boil, turn off the heat and let sit for an hour before returning to a boil and cooking until nearly tender. This may take 1½–2 hours. Do not add salt until beans are cooked. We like to add a 5" piece of kombu (kelp) while cooking to help tenderize the beans and help with digestion.

Directions

Drain the cooked beans and mash them. Add water as needed so that they are moist but not soupy. Minced garlic, ground cumin, chili powder can be added at the end of cooking, but these beans are fine with only a little salt.

Vegan Cheese Dip
Makes 2 cups

Ingredients
2 cups water
⅓ cup nutritional yeast flakes
¼ cup tahini
¼ cup kudzu or flour
2 tablespoon lemon juice
1 tablespoon onion powder or fresh minced onion
1 teaspoon salt
Dash or two turmeric, for color
2 dashes liquid smoke
2 jalapeno peppers, minced
3 tablespoons red bell peppers, minced

Directions
Mix all ingredients. Place in a medium saucepan and bring to a boil, stirring constantly until thick. Remove from heat and serve.

To serve:
Any fresh vegetable from the garden makes a good filling addition. We place all the choices out in pretty bowls on the table so guests can choose their own fillings. Our favorites include lettuce, tomatoes, onions, hot and green peppers, cucumbers, fresh cilantro, celery, tender beet and kale greens.

Dolmas
(stuffed grape leaves)
Makes 60 dolmas. Serving size 4-6 per person.

A lot of people say Kathy makes the best stuffed grape leaves they've ever tasted. A couple of weeks ago she cooked up a batch of them for the girls from work who came up late afternoon for "Happy Hour." We go right out to the vines and pick the leaves. I let a fox grape (wild grape) grow up one of the windmill's guy wires just for that purpose.

Grape leaves all ready to stuff are available in many grocery stores. If picking your own you want to choose leaves that are tender and about 4 to 5-inches across. Since preparing dolmas is something of a labor-intensive process, we make a big batch of and eat them out of the fridge for days. This is a great dish for a party. The recipe can be halved if you don't want such a large number of dolmas.

Ingredients
   60 grape leaves, store-bought or homegrown

Filling Ingredients
   2½ cups short grain brown rice (makes 5 cups cooked rice)
   1 cup chopped parsley
   ½ cup chopped onion
   2 cloves minced garlic
   ½ cup sunflower seeds
   ½ cup raisins
   1 tablespoon oregano or basil
   1 teaspoon salt
   1 teaspoon black pepper

Cooking sauce ingredients
   ¾ cup olive oil
   ½ cup fresh lemon juice
   1 cup water

Directions

1. If using homegrown grape leaves, pick about 60, plunge them into boiling water for about 4-5 minutes. Remove, rinse in cold water and set aside.
2. Prepare rice according to package. Cool. In a bowl, combine all the filling ingredients and set aside.
3. Prepare cooking sauce. Mix sauce ingredients in a tight-fitting jar and shake until blended. Set aside.

To assemble:

1. Place a grape leaf in front of you with the shiny side down and the stem end nearest to you. Snip the stem to about ¼ inch. Place a rounded teaspoon of filling near the stem, fold the stem over the filling, then fold the two ends towards the filling, and finally roll the leaf tightly and away from you.
2. Place the rolled grape leaf, stem side down, in a large, heavy casserole or pan. Continue rolling in this manner until leaves and/or filling is used.
3. Pour cooking sauce over the grape leaves in the pan. Cook either in the oven at 350°F or on top of the stove, until simmering. Baste with juice from the bottom of the pan every 10-15 minutes. Cook 1½-2 hours.

Dolmas can be frozen or sent through a canning process, but they'll last a good week in the refrigerator.

Halloween Soup

Serves 6–8

Kathy cooks two dishes for their holiday color. One is Peas Paneer, which she cooks for Christmas. You'll find a recipe for that in every East Indian cookbook. The other is her Halloween Soup. The main ingredients are our homegrown black beans and carrots (black and orange for Halloween).

Ingredients
  2 cups dry black beans (Wash and pick through beans for any dirt clumps or small stones.)
  6 cups water
  2 cups sliced carrots
  ½ cup chopped celery
  ½ cup chopped onion
  2 cloves chopped garlic
  Olive oil for the sauté pan
  2 teaspoons cumin
  1 teaspoon salt, or to taste
  1 teaspoon pepper, or to taste

Directions
1. Cook beans as in the recipe for the tortilla filling, above. Set aside.
2. Sauté carrots, celery, onion and garlic in a little olive oil until tender. Add this to the bean pot, along with cumin and salt and pepper to taste. Cook for 30 minutes or so, until beans and carrots are tender.

Mamaw's Strawberry Pie
Makes one 8- or 9-inch pie

When you make baklava – having shelled your own butternuts, hickory nuts and black walnuts (and you use red maple syrup to ooze out the phyllo dough instead of traditional honey) – you basically take a peek into heaven from the East. Likewise, your first couple of bites of Mamaw's strawberry pie gives you a view of heaven from the West. Then when you've eaten yourself catatonic you just lie there in misery sprawled out on the couch with a tiny but meaningful glimpse into overeater's purgatory.

I called Kathy's mom Mamaw. She passed away some years back. There's only one trouble with this pie and it doesn't take a genius to figure out what it is (hint: how to put the fork down and say, "Enough"). Back in 1941, Mamaw used a diary to handwrite her recipes and this is one of them. This pie is good without the whipped cream and sweeter without the lemon juice.

The great advantage of having a large strawberry patch of our own is that we can hand pick a quart of perfectly formed, perfectly ripe berries for the pie.

Ingredients
    1 baked piecrust
    1 quart hulled strawberries, washed and drained
    ¾ cup water
    3 tablespoons cornstarch
    1 cup sugar
    1 teaspoon fresh lemon juice
    1 cup heavy cream, whipped and sweetened

Directions

1. Line cooled piecrust with berries, reserving ½ cup for glaze.

2. In a saucepan, simmer whole reserved berries with water for 3-4 minutes.

3. Combine cornstarch and sugar and add to berries in saucepan. Cook until syrup is thick and clear, stirring constantly. Add lemon juice. Cool slightly, then pour glazed berries over berries in prepared piecrust and chill thoroughly. Decorate with border of sweetened whipped cream.

Kathy and Heidi, both hard at work

15

The Years Ahead of Us

*"In reality, both consciously and subconsciously, everything I've done
has been geared to an easy, self-sustaining retirement."*

＆ip

Two people I know of inspire me toward my retirement years.
One was Scott Nearing, who I never had the privilege of
meeting. He died in 1983 at the age of 100. The other person
is my 86-year-old buddy Wray. Both these guys kept an active
lifestyle on into their old age. Wray still cuts his own firewood
but he doesn't garden like he used to.

Scott and his wife Helen wrote the self-sufficiency classic,
"Living the Good Life" (1954). It's about living in simplicity
on their "forest farm" in Vermont, somewhat similar to our forest farm. Much of the labor in their younger years was geared
toward preparing for their latter years, one example being the
great slip-form stone wall that surrounds their garden. It was
a permanent solution to their deer pest problem, done with no
upkeep, no rebuild – done once and for all. It was built in the

years when they could handle the 80-plus pound sacks of Portland cement so they wouldn't have a problem when age prevented them from lifting that much.

Here at The Stone Camp we have a deer pest problem as well and have tried various ways of addressing it, none of them foolproof or ultimately deer-proof. As opposed to a slip-form stone wall, and from my own experience, the permanent solution I've decided on is the Spanish hacienda inner court approach. It involves linking the many structures with double height chain link fence (with massive steel posts sunk in concrete) to include the gardens, orchard, vineyard and berry patches. That will be my permanent, done with, no upkeep and no rebuild solution.

I grew up observing the repercussions from a "good enough for now" approach to things. For that reason I tend to design "good enough forever" into most of my endeavors. The gray water, methane, alcohol distillery and wood gasifier are permanent, like the Nearings' slip-form wall. These, along with the icehouse plans, are lifetime designs.

As we streamline our routines, every year the work gets easier and easier. Now it feels like half the effort it once was, even though we're half again as old as when we started out.

You know, when a child is growing up, his growth goes through relatively proportionate stages. One arm doesn't suddenly grow long and mature before the other one. All his fingers toes, ears and legs mature in a somewhat balanced unison. That's kind of like me pondering and working on 35 project extremities at once.

Then all of a sudden seven of the projects complete themselves and it's like the kid just turned 15. Then he switches from junior high to senior high, goes on his first date and starts to anticipate getting his driver's license. That's a big change, but he's still got a way to go till he reaches maturity.

Right now I have just three projects, maybe four, to complete and then I think this place will reach its mid-adulthood, worthy of a coming-out party for the Independent Self-Sufficient Self-Sustaining Lifestyle. What happens after that is just icing on the cake, or like the midlife hobbies and changes that occur before you wake up and realize your kids are here to spoon feed you breakfast.

Of those projects, one is already complete (the alcohol fuel still), two are 90% complete (the methane digester/storage facility and a new greenhouse for Kathy), and the last is about 20% (the icehouse). But why stop there? While I'm completing these main projects, I've involved both thought and deed to switching the sawmill from its own engine power plant to instead run off the many PTO's (power take-offs) on my many tractors. I'm also adapting the mobile, steel-wheeled 6-ton stone crusher to be pulled by one of the track machines, because a mule train of three rubber-tired farm tractors can't even pull it out of its own shadow. Then there's the Finnish sauna. I just brought it up from where it was originally built, down by the stream a half-mile below, and I'm prepping a foundation for it. It's fully operational, but it's sitting here temporarily on a dual axle trailer waiting for that foundation. Other things that are circling around in my thoughts: sowing cover crops, drying pears, bottling wine, upgrading the electric system…and just now seeing that this particular tangent could easily turn into another book.

Granted, in my later years I won't be going out busting ass on firewood, bringing in two cords a day by myself. I'll stretch it out like Wray does. For years I split with a maul and wedges and now I have a couple of options to do it mechanically with a 3-point hitch hydraulic splitter and one of those PTO splitting screws.

Kathy looks forward to retiring and gardening full time, from summer crops to growing winter salad greens in her free-standing sun pit greenhouse that's almost completed. It adjoins the main garden, right off the edge of the patio and will have a liquid heat storage reservoir. I built one for some friends who grew lettuce and spinach all winter long. I look forward to trying my hand at exotic fruits like figs, dwarf bananas, oranges, lemons, and limes and finally getting around to reading Thoreau and Emerson, since so many people have assumed they inspired me.

In reality, both consciously and subconsciously, everything I've done has been geared to an easy, self-sustaining retirement. I envision our retirement as a mindless routine that requires as little reflection, concern and decision-making as possible. I look forward to going off to hunt mushrooms on my Honda 90 street/trail converted to alcohol, to taking the mini-camper van to Dolly Sods Wilderness Area to pick huckleberries and cranberries.

I've been a vegetarian for 37 years, but man, do I miss fishing for trout. I do all this gathering of nuts and berries, but there's no thrill of the hunt. My favorite activity of all is long midnight journeys through the full-moonlit forest for a ninja night of illegal fish poaching. I tried eating fish a couple times, mainly so I could justify getting back into poaching a dinner or two, but it upset my digestion and I'm really not comfortable ending sentient life. However, if the need arises and I'm hungry for fish, your alarms, trespass signs and fences are in vain. You've been warned.

As I look ahead, I see our life enveloped in bliss, driven by a perfect balance of effort and effortlessness. A life that's as free of worldly stock market concerns as possible. The future holds a lot of mystery and excitement for us. If all goes well with us, we have a number of years to finish our dream and give it a coat of varnish.

We envision having a nice vernal pond with lily pads deep enough for a dive. We want to listen to bullfrogs and feed a couple of those koi fish and maybe have a turtle or two. Kathy has always wanted her very own "duckies" to love and take care of. We plan on a large utility room built on the northern side of the house, and to be able to completely encircle the house with a screened-in porch, deck and patio.

We may even go backward. I'm planning an elevator on the windmill tower but we may decide to give up the entire electric/ electronic world altogether – pedal a bike to wash our clothes and light the house with alcohol and methane. I'd always have the big tractor-driven alternator to weld with and I can run power tools on a smaller alcohol-burning generator. Who knows? I'm driving to town today. I might get hit by a semi truck that lost its brakes coming down the mountain. Who knows?

All I know is I tried like hell to see through the snake oil and think for myself, and this independent off-grid self sufficient lifestyle is what I came up with. We did it at poverty level too. We have our million-dollar dream like everybody else. I often think of what I could do if I could wave a magic wand and command a host of talented salaried people to do my bidding and not be so restricted by a lack of funds. That dream is something like Camelot come to life. It would be the integration of man's greatest DIY ideas in gardening and sustainability – but sorry, no bio-dome, space flight or teasing the nuclear death adder. My dream is so huge and complex in its profound simplicity it would take yet another whole book just to describe it.

When I see rich people build great elaborate tributes to vanity that are an insult to the poverty stricken – when I see people get heavily funded to do a great big "What's the point?" project – I think to myself, I could build something just as great and elaborate that would give hope and inspiration to the poor, something that would destroy envy instead of feeding it. The snake oil salesman came offering an upwardly mobile cure to our misery, but his lies have fangs that inflict venomous bites on the limbs of our very soul. Once in our bloodstream the venom eats away at our spirit. What is the anti-venom? Seeing the world's peer pressure shit for what it is. And thinking for yourself. That's the cure and the immunity.

One thing I hear a lot when people come to visit is, "Now I see how much I have to learn." At first I wasn't so quick witted, but now I point out straightway, "No, it's not that at all. Now you see how much you have to unlearn." Maybe that really is what this book has been about, teaching a process of unlearning so that you can come to your own clear vision for the future.

Kathy joins me in wishing you well. I hope I've given you something to consider by showing you how we live up here at The Stone Camp – and perhaps more important, why we've made the choices we've made. May you create your own life of comfortable, thoughtful independence. And may it bring you true contentment.

Teddy and Kathy

EPILOGUE

Wilderness is not a luxury but a necessity of the human spirit.
It is not enough to understand the natural world;
the point is to defend and preserve it.
– EDWARD ABBEY

ON FORESTS, WOOD GASIFICATION AND TRUE SUSTAINABILITY

"I know of no life form that strives to be weak and sickly,
that willfully and irretrievably gives up its own vitality."

&p;

I heard that once upon a time a squirrel could travel from coast to coast on tree limbs. I've also read some of the written accounts of the first explorers – of a pristine, humbling, inspiring majesty. A stable majesty. So, just who was managing those forests back then when they achieved such sustained equilibrium? I know one thing: It wasn't the timber industry and its schools of forestry management.

I used to be a logger. My family has been five generations working in the woods. I've worked for helicopter loggers, high lead loggers and I'm still the sawyer on the family's sawmill. I also worked for the National Forest Service and dated the daughters of high-ranking G12-G14's in the Forest Service. That meant I picnicked with the biggies. Vast clear cuts were ordered by their signatures. I both heard and was led to believe every rational justification for cutting down healthy trees. I heard the science ones, the math ones, the ecological/economical ones, mostly from the forestry department – and then I got my ears so full of the Paul Bunion macho man ones from my logger friends that I too started walking around macho, with my "Loggers World" suspenders (they now hang on the back of a shed door with a tree hugger pin attached to them).

But these folks aren't the cause of our forest policies, they're just the symptom of placing a prejudicial claim upon what is the forest's own wisdom to manage itself. They became the management messengers of a timber industry – "management" being a word that's been systematically abused until, in practice, it means just the opposite.

I'm not alone in the belief that our commonwealth, our state and national forests and lands, should be as sacred as a church service. Untouched wilderness has the power to render us speechless. It jerks an egocentric thought process right off its throne. That's the therapy that the saints, mystics and seers sought out. The untouched wilderness simply *is*. It is one without a second. It is for impression, to be observed but not scrutinized. Its silence has a voice that speaks immunity to biased and partisan opinions, which in truth have no substance. Opinion only arises when its *is*-ness, its very being, is made to become other than it is, or to serve some supposed utility or purpose. And so we have untouched wilderness being scrutinized to serve special interest narcissism – without modesty, let alone reverence.

I'm not advocating for a completely fallow policy regarding the commonwealth and its resources. These common lands can serve a common cause in other ways. And I'm not referring to all

the token sustainability you hear from everybody and his timber/
gas/oil company brother. True sustainability is a two-way street.
For the commonwealth lands to serve us, we must serve them
equally. Gardeners know the importance of amending the soil. If
they don't amend they don't eat. The more they amend the more
they get to eat and the more organically they amend, the tastier
and more nutritious their food becomes.

If we as cultivating doctors tended to and enhanced the majesty and equilibrium of our commonwealth back to the Lewis
and Clark experience, we would find that our collective human
experience would likewise intensify, rarify and be distilled to
clear essence. When that happens another magic would begin to
grow and manifest. We would hear the unique and the common
aspects of humanity knocking at the door of the dance studio
instead of the gun store. They'd turn the arsenal to plowshares
and take dancing lessons so they could learn to stop stepping on
each other's feet.

Forestry Management

Schools of forestry management not only claim the forest has to
be "man" managed, they also claim the wisdom to do the managing. That's an audacious step in front of the primordial wisdom that the explorers witnessed. Look at our forests now. Look
directly at what their presumption has done. See their dollar-
sign profit-based pseudo wisdom superimposed on the primordial forest's state of equilibrium. We can still have that majestic
experience, but in God-knows-what tiny percent of the land. We
have the California redwoods, some patches of national forest,

including our own Cook Forest in Pennsylvania. It's even right here not 200 yards from my house. There, on the land borders, are oaks that take the linked arms of two and a half people to wrap around them. These giant oaks are still striving, which begs the question, just how sound is this "maturity" reference point by which the timber industry has defined a tree? These oaks are not anomalies, they are testimonies to what could be and in fact should be. These particular oaks owe their existence to a thin line that remains untouched owing to a border disputation. Absent the dispute, those oaks too would just be a memory.

It is the wealth generated from the first intense timber cull that both founded and funded most schools of forestry in most universities. What gets taught in these hallowed halls is not holistic. It's designed to justify and serve a particular way of "seeing" a tree. It appears to stand to logic, but because it starts with a false and limited premise it can only lead to a false and limited conclusion. The wilderness must be permitted to regain strength. It must be allowed to exist free of our mistaken dominance. Silence is its voice. Through attuning your ear to silence its voice is heard. That voice will clarify who we really are and give peace to our struggle. Nature holds the spiritual and scientific answers to all mysteries. Answering all questions, it promotes an all-healing. The mystery must remain a mystery until we cease our exploits and prove ourselves worthy to embrace, serve and be its steward. We would be wise to care for what wilderness remains, as if it literally contained the last vestige of our sanity.

Ruth Scott always advocated that everyone culture a portion of wilderness in the corner of their lawn. I advocate so doing and even to expand it to the end that there is no lawn, but rather half garden and half wilderness. We should make this wilderness portion a classroom curriculum for both our children and ourselves. I'd call the curriculum "The Invisible Presence: How to Walk in Nature Without Leaving Tracks 101." If you want to raise a balanced child in this unbalanced world teach it wilderness sensitivity. Though the wilderness is a woven tapestry of sheer diversity, she is one living entity. She is the closest we can come to the voice and flesh of the one God. She is now responding to our abuse of her, but she will also respond to our love. She is forgiving as God forgives. Our lost self-respect is found in her womb.

Equilibrium and the Three-Part Pie that is a Forest

I think of the forest as a pie cut into thirds. There are three parties with a vested interest, and the forest manifests three distinct aspects. The interested parties are: #1, the forest itself; #2, its wildlife dependants; and #3, man. The three aspects of the forest are: #1, the forest's own health, vitality and majesty – what constitutes its stability and equilibrium; #2, the food, crop and shelter available and utilized by wildlife; and #3, the dead, dying, damaged, blow-down and diseased wood – what we refer to as its "worthless" off-castings.

I know of no life form that strives to be weak and sickly, that willfully and irretrievably gives up its own vitality. The primary interest of any life form is its own strength, stability and equilibrium. Therefore we could say that aspect #1 (the health equilibrium and vitality) belongs to interested party #1, the forest itself. It is the forest's third of the pie. It's obvious that the wildlife (party #2) depends upon aspect #2, which is all that produces both food crop and shelter. So there's only one remaining aspect (the off-castings) and one remaining party (man) left; you do the math.

This off-casting portion of the pie is ours, no more, no less. What the timber companies see as worthless is really both adequate and sufficient to meet our needs. It is the only interest we have a right to collect. If shed by a healthy forest, to which vitality and majesty is given full precedence, then the off-casting is the manna for us to gather.

Wood gasification – which I advocate, both for the energy it produces and for the sustainability it embodies – is an interest/aspect matchup. It is one way of gaining a benefit while at the same time enhancing and safeguarding the forests' majesty, health, depth, resistance and vitality. If wildlife is allotted its slice of the pie, it is a perfect practice.

Special interests in general see themselves deserving of what should be preserved. Is it possible that they and we could both learn to find sustenance in the pie slice allotted to us? I'm sure of it, because I have still have faith in the human spirit.

I find it interesting that both John Muir and Henry Thoreau said something to the effect that you can have this guy that was born in a city. He grew up there, never left the concrete jungle and the only trees he ever saw were planted intermittently along the sidewalk. Yet, as the vitality of the wilderness is diminished, both the look on his face and the quality of his own inner city life is diminished likewise.

If the root of a plant is systematically damaged – if it is neglected, poisoned, decimated – does not the plant itself suffer likewise? The wilderness is the root of human civilization. It is the root of human culture as well. Each of us sprang from it. The definition of sanity is mental balance. An evolved culture that recognizes its own root is mentally balanced. One that separates itself from that recognition can only grow more and more imbalanced.

Our piece of the forest pie can sustain us but it cannot fodder and feed vanity, arrogance and pretense. Prime oak toilet seats, veneer, #1 and #2 grade lumber and knot-free fetishes are all examples, and are unsustainable. I'm aware of wood in all of its uses and states. Seeing grade oak used in a throwaway fast food restaurant is an abomination to the sensitive eye.

Here's an experiment you can try. Take two finished boards. The first one is a low-grade piece, harvested as off-casting and with a few knots and grain irregularities. Then set it beside one "perfect" board. See what your eyes do. If you're seeing more beauty in the "imperfect" board, that's your intuition voicing the truth. It's telling you that the "perfect" board belongs in the tree. Because the character of the "imperfect" board is pleasing and entertaining to the eye, it is intuitively sanctioned as our piece of the pie.

The Perfect Board

Of all the lumber I've sawn in my life, most of it I used or bartered. I only sold a couple thousand board feet of poplar once to a processing plant. My buddy Bruce and I cut the poplars, sawed them and sold them as a joint venture. We both admitted later that it was a mistake and we should have kept and used it ourselves to build things.

When the grader came to our mill to grade the poplar he told us a story that made me sick. He worked for a big facility that buys lumber from most of the mills around. He was grading a bunch of ash wood one morning and came upon a perfectly grained board. It was so unusually perfect that he was moved to set it out and show the guys at lunch.

It happened that a rich Japanese client flew in that day to buy Pennsylvania hardwood for an office building. One of the big bosses was walking this client through the facility and he happened to see this ash board leaning against the wall. He turned to the big boss and said, "I want the whole order in this." The boss kinda chuckled a bit and said, "You have to understand that's damn near impossible." The rich client turned, didn't crack a smile and said, "But not impossible."

If the ash tree had a spirit, or there was like a single spirit of the ash tree, can you imagine what it may have felt at that moment? In the Old Testament there's a story about a people whose culture sort of went down the tubes. Their whole world collapsed for some reason and there was a verse that said, "And the trees rejoiced because now no feller came up against them."

As the space shuttle floated past our continent, the astronauts looked down and saw a particularly verdant patch in northern Minnesota. It intrigued them so much that they inquired about it. Turns out it was the Menomonee Indian Reservation and the vibrancy that was visible from space was due to their timber harvesting practice. I believe this illustrates a rare instance where man takes his proper slice of the forest. It stood out from space!

The Menomonee recognize that the interest of the forest is its own health and vitality, so they don't take bites from that slice. Instead, they harvest the off-castings, the diseased, the injured, the blow-downs. Those are the aspects that don't compete with the forest's desire to regain its majesty and equilibrium. Their consumption enhances the forest's majesty. The Menomonee people culture the forest's pre-white state of being. I am not sure how or even if they consider the wildlife, but it is impressive that the result of their practice was so apparent from space.

Wood Smoke Exhaust

I believe in that sort of timber management and very strongly in wood gasification. Wood smoke isn't an angel and it's not a silver bullet, but I take issue with those who put wood smoke and fossil fuel exhaust under the same ominous heading. Wood smoke exhaust and fossil fuel exhaust have just a single word in common. They're both exhaust, but they're as different as night is to day, organic to inorganic, bioactive to inert, digestible to indigestible; as different as what incense is to noxious diesel exhaust, water soluble is to solvent soluble, and as what dissipates and re-assimilates fully is to what concentrates its byproducts in our organs and gives us cancer.

Wood smoke is fully digestible to the ecosystem, not to

mention its CO_2 release is both inevitable and organic. It is contained in the circle/cycle of life. Like a log rotting away to nothing, it completely re-assimilates back into the living cycle. Even if there is a sudden excess of wood smoke it really does dissipate, get re-absorbed, does minimal harm and seeks balance.

Stubborn Assumptions

When you start hearing forestry experts saying, "The trees are ours for the taking and damn, they must be taken lest a resource goes to waste," you know the insane me-first rationalizing has gone viral and systemic. A young woman I knew who went to a prominent forestry school had strong environmental beliefs. She said she felt like she was always under threat in an ideological war zone – that if you dared utter a voice of environmental concern for the trees or the forest's wildlife dependents you got hazed, called every derogatory "tree hugger" name in the book. The uncompromising righteous attitude, the unwillingness to be challenged are signs to be concerned about. Is it not wiser perhaps to accept that some amount of what we currently accept as truth, even accept as normal, may one day be found based upon some lie or misconception? I heard that when the Dean of Harvard Medical School gives his freshman speech he says, "Welcome to Harvard. Fifty percent of what you're going to be taught here, research will one day prove to be completely wrong. The trouble is we don't know which fifty percent." I would say that's about the best thing you can tell anybody. It would sure as hell work to check the presumptions I see coming out of the forestry schools. And it's not just in forestry, it manifests in every profession. It often takes a steady, incontrovertible drumbeat of new ideas and new data to finally tip the scales of an old way of thinking and give the next iteration of thought a chance. A case in point: The cutting edge of forest pathology no longer teaches or believes in the "mature trees" paradigm. Having no doubt opened their minds to what the forest was and what it has now become, they have shifted to the concept of "the forests' equilibrium." Equilibrium was what the explorers witnessed. You might say it was God's wisdom let to manage the forest, before the lustful eyes of hungry men jumped the cafeteria line to presume that wisdom. What kind of equilibrium can be achieved through modern forest management remains to be seen.

A What-If

The deep frontiers are all but gone at this point. All state and national forests are completely encircled by civilization and most are easily accessed. There are now many small towns at the bases of most federal foothills and mountain ranges and there are people living on the borders of all of our state commonwealth lands.

So pick a park, any park. Then imagine if you would, my dream of two woodgas-fueled generating plants on wheels placed on opposite sides of the park. Now set them to moving slowly from town to town in a clockwise circle that circumnavigates the park. Set them to do it forever; that's what sustainability means. It means constant and forever (what fossil fuels are not).

Woodgas electric plants feeding into a common pool (the grid) would be as sustainable, enriching and as good for the commonwealth as you can get. In each town they stop, plug into the main grid and begin generating electrical power from the off-castings gathered. The very stuff that once ignited, spread in a hot wind and then burned through their town now pays their rent, their food and their electric bill. And how does the off-cast and blow-down wood get to these new power plants? I'd like to see ads everywhere that read:

Help wanted: Forest Groomers
Delicate, careful, low-impact piecework.
Thin the forest and gather waste wood.
Get paid money by the pound
Sanity by the hour
And health by the minute.

Permitted are:
Pack ponies or burros
(either live or battery driven).
All motorized units must be heavily muffled.
Light track machines on 9-plus inches of snow.
All wagons and transports tires must be bald
(inflated 15 psi max).
Must comply with scheduling.
Manual or electric saws only.
Big, fat, belligerent earth ripping log skidders need not apply.

I'm talking about self-regulating piece work – honest, cautious and respectful labor. The harder you work, the more you get paid. You tell me who loses? I see fat shed, forest fire catastrophes avoided, disease checked, and forests restored to pristine health and majesty. And an increased sensitivity to the natural world.

I see truly sustainable jobs where nobody is ever laid off. Why? Because the forest sheds this off-casting fuel source at a constant pace, as opposed to the once-every-60-year timber boom-rape cycle. That boom-rape cycle makes a few men really rich, but it's just the fat worm with its ass in its mouth working its own endeavors.

Like Martin Luther King, I want to say, "I too have a dream." I dream of the end of all special interest exploitation in our state and national commonwealth lands, not only the end of timber, gas, oil and mineral exploitation, but also any motorized recreational vehicle exploitation. I dream that the same rules of behavior that govern sensitive wilderness areas apply to all state and federal lands because that's the only way to guarantee every person a common experience of their very own commonwealth. That's why I dream of erasing roads into the wilderness areas as opposed to building more of them. Personally, I'd pay $500 for a commonwealth entrance certification degree. I'd pay it to learn wilderness sensitivity, fire safety and to have a "pack it in, pack it out" mindset drilled so deep into my brain I couldn't forget it if I wanted to.

The scars of exploitation left by logging, mining, drilling and motorized recreational vehicles at play may not offend the folks who are doing it, but it's not okay with me. In fact, I think the sight of their decimation offends way more people than not. I think the majority of commonwealth citizens are quite taken aback by the blemishes of disrespect than say, "Isn't that nice!"

Common and *special* are words that are diametrically opposed to one another. They are hard pressed to coexist in the same line of thought and that begs one big "elephant in the room" question: What the hell are *special* interests doing in the state and federal *common*wealth? Who gave them permission to exploit the natural resources? I, the common man, did not. And who's saying that these resources have to be exploited in the first place?

I think special interests gave special interests their own permission to exploit the common wealth and it appears they use a good measure of guile, subtlety and deception to gain their advantageous rights to exploit commonwealth resources. Like a cat scratching a tree or a dog pissing on its borders, every special interest both has and leaves its special mark. The scars of exploitation left by logging, mining, drilling and motorized recreational vehicles at play may not offend the ones doing the pissing and the scratching. Now we're in the midst of a gas exploration gold rush, and there's a whole lot of effort to make it appear benign: "Wow, doesn't this drilling platform way out here in the middle of the forest really look nice. We even plant certain wildflowers and mow it with a lawn mower!" They're hoping I won't look at the big-picture abomination and see that it's oozing frack water in my neighbor's well.

It is a vicious cycle of resource exploitation generating big bucks and the big bucks in turn lobbying and buying their way into the political machine. Then with their foothold in government bureaucracy, they gain more permission to exploit more resources.

Trees and Drought: The Acceleration of Elements

When I'm talking with someone about some of the reasons we'd better start managing our forests in a more enlightened way, I like to bring up the subject of floods and drought. It's not usually the first thing people think about when they think of forests. What do forests have to do with those natural disasters? A whole lot, because trees are the water regulators of the ecosystem. For example, their heavily matted root systems absorb and hold water, slowing and controlling the runoff so it can seep into and replenish the ground table. All trees draw moisture up from the ground, store and then slowly transpire into the atmosphere, but a mature tree is like a standing reservoir. The amount of moisture it draws up and regulates can be in the thousands of gallons per day.

To remove these regulators is akin to cutting big holes in a dam. Thus we see the increase in the number of rivers and creeks that reach destructive flood stage while at the same time the water tables are diminishing. The trees that once managed to balance the inflow and outflow of water by storing and releasing it aren't there any more. The acceleration of the element of water has a domino effect on all the other elements because nature is a single organism. Just as a cancer in a single organ eventually affects all organs, the acceleration of the water cycle by cutting timber can affect ambient temperature, wind speed, drought and torrent as well as elements that don't even seem to relate.

So what are we doing when we have government policies that make sure it's completely legal for loggers to knock on the doors of landowners and say, "You know, the best thing you can do for your forest is to cut it completely down."

Yesterday is Today

Rachel Carson, in accepting the Burroughs Medal for her 1952 environmental masterwork, "The Sea Around Us," stated:

"Mankind has gone very far into an artificial world of his own creation. He has sought to insulate himself, in his cities of steel and concrete, from the realities of earth and water and the growing seed. Intoxicated with a sense of his own power, he seems to be going farther and farther into more experiments for the destruction of himself and the world."

Since biblical days we've had our prophets to point out the ways we deceive ourselves and follow down destructive pathways, usually out of ignorance but too often out of greed. It's easy to look at past generations and shake our heads at our ancestors' naiveté and lack of sophistication. But if you had been there, would you not see that they were exactly as we are this very moment? At least half of our history seems to be made up of a series of endeavors that ended in catastrophe. We applaud them at first, only to find out that we just compounded an even greater nightmare.

We don't want to have to wake up one day, look around at our barren hills, blighted air and sickened populations and say, "Oops…whose idea was that?"

ON FOSSIL FUELS AND PETROCHEMICALS

"Fossil fuels...speak a language that is foreign to the circle of life."

෯

When a tree dies, falls and hits the ground it's just like us taking a bite of food. The earth chews it up and digests it into food for living plants. Eventually those plants die, decompose back into nutrients and repeat the process. It's called the perfect circle of life wherein every end meets a new beginning.

Nature's digestive tract is a formula of air, pH, moisture, temperature, bugs, worms and microbes. If that formula isn't balanced, things might not fully decompose and there's a chance the tree might turn to coal instead of rich, fertile humus. It could even become peat, but you just correct the imbalance, add the missing factors and the digestion process can resume.

You might say that fossil fuels are the result of indigestion. Coal and oil don't get broken down into a nutrient form that can further growth. They're hard pressed to be re-assimilated, therefore their presence in the ecosystem causes further indigestion. When fossil fuels are introduced into the living biosphere it's like throwing a wrench into the working mechanics of life. Life forms are designed to change, ceaselessly. But what about fossil fuels, which have achieved entropy in a changeless, bio-resistant, inert state? A biologically active life form and a deceased fossilized death form are about as opposite as you can get.

The link of each end to a new beginning is what keeps the circle of organic life complete and unbroken. It's the way the food chain flows, and it offers continuity to the ceaseless organic change that we call life. We see it in the dead tree that turned into humus but we don't see it in a lump of coal

Fossil fuels are an end that has no apparent link to a new beginning, which means they speak a language that is foreign to the circle of life. Coal, oil and gas simply don't interrelate with life. To living things they are harmful, non-essential, toxic irritants. That's no doubt why, by nature's design, they are packaged to stagnate, why there are barriers set between them and us and also why they move slowly and steadily away from us, ever-increasing the thickness of that barrier. Fossil fuels are a collective mummified corpse of a past life cycle that is compressed solid as in coal, or putrefied to an inert state as in oil. Gas is some of what emanates from the unique process they went through. Coal has its own built-in barrier. It's a mummified solid that's somewhat impervious to breakdown and it is not water-soluble. It's on its way to becoming the most impervious solid, a diamond. You can swallow a chunk of coal or put it in a Christmas stocking without killing your kids.

Tar pits and oil are just the opposite. They are liquids that seep, spread, permeate, corrupt and disrupt. They spread like a slow plague. Gas is even worse. It moves quickly and is near impossible to contain. Because it destroys where and what our eyes cannot see, we tend to think it's benign.

We think it's okay to interpret the foreign language of fossil fuels and make them communicate with the biosphere, but it's not okay. We've invented thousands of ways to force petroleum's inert and final end to have many new beginnings in life and we chose to break down coal's natural barrier and turn it into our major economic sustenance. We toss the mummified corpse into a big blast furnace and the whole world is forced to breathe the fumes.

We also alter the chemical makeup of coal and oil and force feed it into nature's digestive tract. We turn them into fertilizers, pesticides and polishes that make things look real good from the outside, but what goes on inside is often a whole different story. Such alchemy goes against the law of nature and we suffer manifold symptoms for transgressing that law. Day by day, as our fossil fuel dependence grows, the repercussions intensify.

I fear the whole idea of a coal/gas/petrochemical industry is like the parable of "a rotten tree being unable to produce good fruit," especially fruit with no toxic side effects.

"unnecessary necessaries"

In the list of necessities that we chose to chemically synthesize from fossil fuel, we always had an organic option. There's aspirin from coal, or there's aspirin from willow tree bark. The plastics, fuels, fertilizers, inks, medications etc., all have their organic, bioactive counterparts. Consider that the prototype gasoline engine is said to have been originally invented to run on alcohol, and the diesel was first designed to run on vegetable oil. I stress the word necessity, because for the most part, those products that don't have an organic counterpart service a long list of just plain unnecessary things. They feed and enrich desires, patronize some pointless vanity or just polish things up real shiny. As my buddy Mark Twain said: "Civilization is a limitless multiplication of unnecessary necessaries."

We breathe in, absorb and ingest synthesized petrochemical compounds every moment of every day. The air looks clean, the food tastes good, but we know for a fact that our own bodies are heavily polluted with these chemical nightmares and we're now finding hundreds of them in the blood of newborn babies. We know that we're dying from the cancers, diseases and birth defects that they cause. Whether we connect these dots or not makes no difference because the dots were never disconnected in the first place.

No doubt chemically-bathed apples are big, uniform, and they don't have spots. No doubt Roundup Ready seed appears as a savior that can save and feed the world. The thing is, something has trained our eyes so they can't focus on the real truth of the matter. It's hard to see with clarity in the face of all those rosy promises of better living through a petroleum-based lifestyle. Now, a clever lawyer can make the truth look like a lie and can make the lie look like the truth. The coal and petrochemical industry can't disprove the obvious truth so they keep a stable full of lawyers specifically hired to shift responsibility. Because it's impossible to prove there's no connection between their synthetics and our disease, they demand that we prove there *is* a connection. That lets them conjure the illusion of a gap between cause and effect that was never there in the first place. It's a damn subtle form of deception that really, really works.

The petrochemical industry knows that the only way to confuse the obvious, whole and complete truth is to drag it down into the realm of divisive thought and argument. Therefore, they succeed only if we accept the challenge to prove there is a connection. However, no law says that we have to accept their challenge. It's not our responsibility to prove that their creations are harmful, it's their responsibility to prove that they are harm*less*.

The industry knows they can't provide that proof. They know they can't win a court case. However, they're well aware that they do achieve their goal if in fact a verdict can't be reached. So they don't seek to win, but only to perpetuate the battle. If there is no winner, if no verdict is reached, then the court must remain in session, hopefully forever on their part. For as long as the court remains in session, the industry is permitted to keep selling their herbicides, pesticides and genetically manipulated abominations. That's the nailhead of a horrific special interest lobbied injustice and it's why the industry is so audacious, threatening and belligerent toward, for example, farmers who don't buy into their lie.

"First flood the market with it and if anybody starts getting sick we'll have to take a closer look at it, maybe even test it." That is an attitude and practice that values you and me as little more than guinea pigs to experiment on. And they gained the permission to practice this deceitful injustice through lobbying Congress and infiltrating government positions. We are told that we have to prove there is a connection between death and death, between your creative, disruptive chemical nightmares and the increased cancer, disease and birth defects that we suffer, when it's really your responsibility to prove there is not.

The Alchemy of Disease

Single living organisms are formed from many cells that combine and integrate their labors. Whether it's as small as an ant or as big as the earth itself, it's just a bunch of cells that organized their workload toward a single goal: sustaining life.

Cells are mindless workers. They don't reflect. Their labors have to be directed. If the chain of command is clear, all happens with ease. If not, they lose directional clarity. In losing sight of the prime directive, cells lose sight of the first order of things, but they don't stop working. They just set out blindly – confused and enthusiastic – in a new direction. When the first chain of command is garbled or blocked, symbiotic integration turns abruptly into divisive disintegration. That's because the energy these cells need to build their tumor and strengthen their new, deluded cause is now drawn from the body and nothing is given back to serve, strengthen and enrich that body. This defines dis-ease. As dis-ease proceeds, signs of war manifest: a tumor forms or there's a sudden drastic change in blood chemistry. In this light, cancer is not so much a random mystery, it's simply a house divided against itself, a single body with two goal posts instead of one.

There's really no line of demarcation between environmental and hereditary causes. Seeking to isolate that line only undermines holistic medical understanding. Cells just pass on their clear or deluded tendencies through our genes. In other words, the environmental sins of the father-body actually can be passed on to the child. The only true healing is to redirect the cells to integrate their labors. You have to get the chemical static out of the system so their orders come through loud and clear. Then with appropriate therapy you have to heal the internal cuts and bruises that the chemicals caused so the cells regain the strength to follow those orders.

The work orders get to the cells through the nerves and their synapses much like electricity does through wires and points of contact. An inert, bio-inactive substance is to life what a non-conductor is to electricity. Clear messages eventually establish synapses around solid things like metal implants or artificial organs, but it's different when flesh, or an organ the message travels through, is chemically saturated. The message gets through, but having just traveled through flesh-turned-chemical-sponge it arrives distorted and confused, deranged by the effects of toxicity. This causes internal factions to arise in the body (disease), and so the body's integrative clarity is lost sight of and ignored. A misconstrued, misinterpreted message is the wrong message. It can be worse than receiving no message at all.

Petrochemicals are easily poured into and absorbed into our bodies, but they can be hard if not impossible to get back out because the body has developed no means to latch onto and expel them. Some pollute the blood and lymph and many eventually saturate our organs where they just build up sediment as behind a dam. When some part of the body does get saturated with a synthesized non-conducting foreign substance, all hell breaks loose. I believe that miscommunication at the cellular level will one day be understood as the heading under which most all disease falls. I can almost guarantee that the flooding of the biosphere with the alchemy of inert fossilized death will one day be identified as the big culprit behind our endless suffering. I'm talking physical and mental as well.

Chimneys and Other Illusions

American Indians referred to coal as "the black rock that burns." It burns longer, hotter and far more efficiently than wood, but still they didn't burn it in their dwellings. Why? No doubt the ones who tried were quick to see the link between its emission and their health. The advent of the chimney severed that direct link between cause and effect. It made us think we could have the warmth and expel the harmful exhaust out there where it won't hurt us.

I had a very sick great uncle. The basement of his house was his garage. In despair one night he closed all the windows, started the car, walked upstairs to his favorite chair, sat down and died. We too live in a closed system, because like my uncle's house, our planet has no open windows. Our atmosphere doesn't vent into outer space. The whole idea that a chimney gets rid of anything is an illusion. There is no elsewhere, no other place for toxins to go but right here. The coal, oil and petrochemical industry influence us to run upwards of a billion cars and light trucks, consume all the power the coal-fired plants can produce and to flood the world with their chemically concocted inventions. We're doing all this in our closed atmospheric bubble and we can't understand why everybody's getting sick and dying.

I said earlier that natural barriers are set between us and the fossilized corpse we call coal and oil. Breaks in that barrier occur both in nature and by our folly, but the repercussions in both cases are disruptive to life. Look at the difference between petroleum venting naturally from the ocean floor and what happens in a human-caused petroleum spill. The largest natural seeps are said to amount to about 50 gallons a day. One of our spills can go into the millions. In either case it has no good effect on the balance of life. Yes, you can find living microbes in a coal seam or an oil pocket, but even they don't interact with the biosphere. Their entire world is an isolated dead zone.

There's not enough room here for me to even begin listing all the ills that befall us because of our deadly embrace of fossil fuels in our lives. But I believe the day will come when enough people will see the truth and we will start to find our way back to ecological balance and health. At the moment, most people continue to support the use of fossil fuels, for whatever reasons. Maybe they work in the coal or oil fields, as I once did, or maybe those companies have done really well for the old stock portfolio. Or there was the camaraderie of being swept up into the "drill baby drill" peer pressure of some group's political or philosophical belief. Or maybe the reason is as simple as the fact that we've grown so comfortable with the short term convenience of fossil fuels that it hadn't occurred to us to question "the way things are." I think that accounts for the greatest number of us.

Sustainability: the Way Back

How do we start to get out from under this fossil fuel/petro-chemical beast that saps our life force and that of the earth? Alternative energies are more than sufficient to supply our needs, but we have to turn out the lights when we leave the room. The hell-bent pursuit of upward mobility and economic growth – excess in general, shifting into overdrive – all serves to blind us to conservative necessity. A switch to alternative energy demands efficiency and the elimination of waste. Such a switch can strongly contribute a check and balance to consumptive desires gone rampant. That would in turn help us regain the stability and health of our support system, the biosphere. It's up to us to clarify and separate desire from clear necessity and establish a new paradigm that really is sustainable.

It is within our imagination to picture us having evolved through a difference set of choices, coming into synch with the laws of providence. Near total localized economies. Immense resistance to catastrophe. Giant sailing ships spreading non-perishable commerce, with no one in a hurry. Every stream and river drinkable. Zero waste. Mental balance.

A healthy, vital, self-sustaining civilization will be the one that sets limits to the pursuit of "unnecessary necessaries." A great Gnani philosopher of India once said: "Nothing profits the world as much as the non-seeking of profit." He also said, "The only evil in the world is what's unnecessary. The only good is the necessary."

On Dominion, Disposability and the Undivided Eye

*"If, despite our preferences or dislikes of any kind, we award
all things a role to play in life, our perception is coming
from one fundamental reference point."*

∽

In light of the things humanity is willing to do to the earth
and to one another, we would appear to be a fundamentally
deranged species. For the Western world it didn't help much
that the King James biblical interpretation gave us the "absolute
dominion" paradigm. In truth, living with that imperative has not
enriched us.   It instead sentences us to suffer extreme spiritual
poverty, even if it takes a long time for us to recognize that that's
what it is.

The idea of our absolute dominion isn't working for us. Look
around – we've been feeding excessively upon our earth. It's a
slow suicide for our culture to remain insensitive and oblivious
toward the very thing that nurtures us, supports us and gives
us life. But we can't seem to wash out the stain of superior and

deserving hues from the suit of "dominion" we were given to wear. Stewardship is the only thing that can get rid of them.

Psychologist and body linguists agree that when a man folds his arms he has postured his defiance, his unwillingness to further consider. Appropriately referring to our condition, one Old Testament prophet proclaimed, "And man folds his arms and eats his own flesh."

Free will is founded upon the idea of choice. In Western religious traditions it's written that humanity was given the option to adhere to one single obedience. The granting of that option was necessary to generate an element of free will, and that gave birth to reason. The story of Eden contained a forewarning. The ramifications and repercussions of both obedience and disobedience were right up front. We were told straight out what basing a mindset on disobedience would turn us into. We would lose our bliss, our Eden, and have to find our way back somehow.

A disobedient mindset is a divisive, disruptive mindset. It has been propelling us on a downward spiral ever since. We are not transcending wars and dissention and abuse of the earth that upholds us. Instead, we seem to have become an environmental, ecological curse upon the land and, increasingly, upon ourselves.

I believe the way back calls on us to find the same balance point of contradiction between dominion and stewardship...the point where the two touch, are in check and they don't lose sight of one another. In knowing both, our eyes and minds become single. I have pondered this for many years and I deeply believe that it is the divided eye that has gotten us to the mess we're in now.

The Divided Eye

I'm going to make a claim that you might find extreme, but you'll see where it's leading. A taproot is the main part of a plant that seeks and becomes the primary channel for both moisture and nourishment. Racist, bigoted thought has a taproot as well, which I've come to realize is sunk deep in what we call the idea of disposability. It starts with the concept of "garbage." I believe that the world suffers bigotry and racism to the very degree it participates in disposability. It's all about the way we think about and consider things other than ourselves.

It's human nature to classify what we perceive into one of two distinct fundamental reference points. If we are acutely aware of our own perceptions we will see that our very first consideration of a thing is the name that defines it. Clinging like glue to that first consideration is our impulse to categorize that single thing into one of these two reference points: What pleases us, serves us, interests us and amuses us becomes our one fundamental reference point, and what doesn't please, serve, amuse or interest us becomes the other. To our likes and preferences we award meaning and worth. To those things we strip of meaning and value we more or less refuse to grant an active part in life's design.

After the initial spontaneous naming and categorizing of a thing, we then go about elaborating our attitude with degrees of preference or intensities of disgust toward that thing. From that we calculate how close we want to keep it or how far to throw it away. It is judgment that slices through and separates our likes from our dislikes and creates the distinction between the two. It is judgment that gives or takes away its value. There is actually a third categorization, which is profound indifference. The Buddhists refer to these as "The Three Poisons."

The disposable mentality, like bigotry, is the mind divided between two reference points. It is a mentality that divides our eye, which in turn divides us from within ourselves. The question is, if we are so highly and completely under the influence of categorization toward all things we perceive, how can we expect ourselves to view people any differently?

Consider terms like "useless," "offensive," "no good," "garbage," "trash," "filth," and "waste." They're all bilateral terms, words of categorized judgment. They describe what we send to the landfill and they flow from the mouth of every racist bigot in reference to his idea of "disposable" people. I'm not claiming that 100% recycling is the messianic answer to our ills, but I won't say that it isn't. What I am saying is that if you eliminate every trace of material disposableness and engage in an economy based on zero waste, you cannot be a bigot. A 100% recycling lifestyle and a racist lifestyle are two opposite realities. They will not fit into one person or one brain.

I've used the word bigot. Dictionaries can't agree on exactly where the word came from in the first place. Since no one else has come up with a derivation that makes any sense, I'd like to offer my own, just for the hell of it.

From the Teddy Carns Dictionary: **Bigot (n.) big-ət, meaning derived (got) from two (bi), representing the end product of a divided eye. Antonym: Uni-got, possessing an undivided eye; able to see all creation as one unbroken unity.**

Recycling is "uni-got." It is the single, undivided eye because its perception allows for only one bottom line: Whether a thing serves me or not is secondary and subservient to the fact that all things have a part to play in life. Even if it has become "useless," smells offensive and has turned ugly, its end comes to face a new beginning. That itself is a single reference point, and it completely undermines bigotry as well as extreme self-interest.

Recycling, this joining of end to beginning, is a primary part of nature's ordinance. But there's a whole lot of refusal going on. Did you ever think about the word "refuse," what we do with our arms folded defiantly? Have you ever connected it with that other word, "refuse" (accent on the first syllable), the stuff we throw away...our garbage? They both originate from the same French word. So first we refuse, then we bag our refuse and toss that end that will have no beginning into the big "refusal" at the landfill.

Nature's Equilibrium

If, despite our preferences or dislikes of any kind, we award all things a role to play in life, our perception is coming from one fundamental reference point. Its bottom line says everything has value – whereas the bottom line of the disposability mindset is divided, judgmental and given to doing great harm. To continue tapping into the landfill, literally and figuratively, is an abomination to our human spirit. "The stone that the builders rejected, the same has become the head of the corner. It is the Lord's work and it is marvelous in our eyes."

So, aside from washing the canvas with the occasional cataclysm, the vitality and majesty of creation has always been fed and sustained by its own weakness and off-castings. Nature never had a landfill mentality. In nature there is no such thing as waste. Natural Law, "survival of the fittest," was established by the Creator to keep creation in tiptop shape. The vitality, strength and stable equilibrium in life were not intended to be culled and consumed in the natural order of things (a case in point is our wholesale exploitation of prime natural resources). View any link in the food chain and you will see that the magnificence of creation was meant to be cultured, nourished, preserved and sustained directly in the consumption of its own deficiencies and weakness – nature's recycling process. In that way, eyes beholding creation would forever look upon sustainable majesty in a state of equilibrium.

Our being at the top of the food chain gave birth to our humanity. It's because there's no predator in the natural order to systematically cull our handicapped, aged, sick and deficient that we became humane. Our call to love, honor and care for our weakness is compassion. That's what gave us the gift and clarity of reason. It's a good thing to remember. All that superiority crap that we glean from the book of Genesis to justify our ecological dictatorship is, in my humble opinion, pure, unadulterated bullshit.

ACKNOWLEDGMENTS

♊

Short of acknowledging every event and thought that has influenced my perception, I would like to thank Kathy (my dear wife) and Cathy (my dear editor). The former for grounding my life, the latter for grounding my words. Also to my right hand man, David Keener, who left the world this March on the eve of his birthday. And thank you to Paul Kelly, my publisher, for his belief in the message of this book.

ABOUT THE AUTHOR

dp

Ted Carns approaches every technical and environmental challenge with a rare kind of creative inventiveness. He and his social worker wife Kathy live in their one-of-a-kind  home on five acres of land, run entirely by alternative fuels and power systems: alcohol, methane, solar/wind electric, wood gasification, biodiesel. With all the comforts and conveniences of the 21st century, theirs is a self-sustaining, simple life that works: zero waste, total recycling, and respectful environmental stewardship. Ted has become an almost mythic figure to the thousands of people who have made the pilgrimage to learn the secrets of the beautiful and astonishing Stone Camp.

Ted and Kathy live in the highlands of western Pennsylvania.

www.thestonecamp.com

CPSIA information can be obtained
at www.ICGtesting.com
Printed in the USA
FSOW01n2241151117
41240FS